"*Is This Really Love?* serves as a vital guide for anyone feeling tossed in the confusing storm of emotional abuse. Skillfully written in the voice of a wise and caring friend, Leah Aguirre offers readers a remarkable gift I will recommend for years."

—**Gina Simmons Schneider, PhD**, psychotherapist, and author of *Frazzlebrain*

"*Is This Really Love?* is a must-read for those who question the health of their relationship or struggle to relate honestly in relationships. Leah Aguirre writes with authority and experience, and guides her reader on a pathway from discernment to recovery and wholeness."

—**Reta Faye Walker, PhD**, founder and executive director of Lasting Love Transformation, and author of *Guide to Lasting Love*

"This book is a must-read for anyone who wants to break the cycle of falling for coercive, controlling, or emotionally abusive romantic partners. With expert research, guidance, and personal stories, Leah Aguirre's book guides readers to heal, reconnect with themselves, and make sure their next relationship is healthy and loving."

—**Lily Womble**, author of *Thank You, More Please*; and founder of Date Brazen

"A clear guide and an anchor of truth for anyone who is looking to understand the nuances of abuse. This book will give words to your experience, while providing practical steps to healing."

—**Grace Stuart**, domestic violence advocate, and host of the *Why She Stayed* podcast

"In *Is This Really Love?*, Leah deftly addresses the serious subject of emotional abuse. Through real-life stories and straightforward guidance, this book helps readers overcome self-doubt and see the reality of an emotionally abusive partner. *Is This Really Love?* is for anyone questioning a relationship's emotional health, and a must-read for clinicians: because therapists must understand the impact of emotional abuse and how to help clients safely leave these relationships."

—**Jodi White, LPC**, therapist, and host of the *Journals of a Love Addict* podcast

Is this really love?

Recognizing when you're in a coercive, controlling, and emotionally abusive relationship—*and how to break free*

Leah Aguirre, LCSW

New Harbinger Publications, Inc.

Publisher's Note

This publication is designed to provide accurate and authoritative information in regard to the subject matter covered. It is sold with the understanding that the publisher is not engaged in rendering psychological, financial, legal, or other professional services. If expert assistance or counseling is needed, the services of a competent professional should be sought.

NEW HARBINGER PUBLICATIONS is a registered trademark of New Harbinger Publications, Inc.

New Harbinger Publications is an employee-owned company.

Copyright © 2025 by Leah Aguirre
New Harbinger Publications, Inc.
5720 Shattuck Avenue
Oakland, CA 94609
www.newharbinger.com

All Rights Reserved

Cover design by Sara Christian

Acquired by Georgia Kolias

Edited by Diedre Hammons

Library of Congress Cataloging-in-Publication Data on file

Printed in the United States of America

27   26   25

10   9   8   7   6   5   4   3   2   1   First Printing

To my dear friends and family—

Thank you for all the unwavering love and support of my personal healing and this project.

To my life partner—

Thank you for showing me what healthy love looks and feels like and for loving me unconditionally.

Contents

	Foreword	vii
	Introduction	1
Chapter 1	The Nuance of Subtle Abuse	6
Chapter 2	Understanding the Emotionally Abusive Partner	16
Chapter 3	How It Feels to Be in a Relationship with an Emotionally Abusive Partner	24
Chapter 4	Escaping the Fantasy and Acknowledging the Reality	38
Chapter 5	Leaving Your Emotionally Abusive Partner	53
Chapter 6	Recognizing the Aftereffects of Emotional Abuse	71
Chapter 7	Challenging Your Negative Core Beliefs	85
Chapter 8	Taking Time to Heal	99
Chapter 9	Finding Empowerment	114
	Conclusion: Moving Forward with Intention	129
	Acknowledgments	131
	References	133
	About the Author	135

Foreword

Abuse is insidious. It starts out very gradually, slowly creeping its way into the relationship, incognito. You may find yourself questioning why you feel crazy in your relationship or wondering why your partner seems consistently happy when you're sad, or picking fights with you when you're celebrating a success. Perhaps you are experiencing this nagging feeling that your partner does things to spite you or to take you down a notch. *But, that doesn't make sense. Why would my partner want to do that? Maybe I am just paranoid*, you wonder. Perhaps your physical health has declined over the years; internally, you're in a perpetual state of hypervigilance and stress. Or maybe your partner accuses you of having ill intentions or being unfaithful and you find yourself constantly needing to defend yourself against—what? You don't really know... Feelings of defeat and powerlessness take over as you slip further and further away from your former self.

Unless abuse is overt (i.e., physical abuse, name-calling, etc.), it is often difficult for the person on the receiving end to understand the mistreatment or to understand why they feel so bad in their relationship. Repeated self-blame is an attempt to keep the peace in the relationship, acquiescing in an attempt to make the relationship go back to what it once was. As your own spark fades away, so do your other relationships. Maybe the other people in your life can't stand how your partner treats you or maybe they believe that your partner is the best thing that's ever happened to you. Or perhaps you withdraw from your support system because you are depressed or you are too worn out to deal with the fight you know will arise when you tell your partner that you want to spend time with your family or friends. In any event, you find yourself more alone than ever before. Why can't you just snap out of it? Focus on the good things about your partner? Ignore the complete emotional devastation and humiliation inside when your partner mockingly degrades you in front of others?

The inner turmoil experienced from an emotionally abusive relationship is exhausting, depleting, and all-consuming. *Is This Really Love?* is a beautiful guide to help you identify whether or not your relationship is emotionally abusive. Leah gives case studies and clear examples of common experiences in emotionally abusive relationships, shedding light on normally hard-to-see patterns. This book also provides thought-provoking exercises to help you reconnect to yourself and your real needs, identify unhealthy aspects of your relationship, and learn how to recover.

For a long time the image of what you thought your relationship was going to be keeps you working really hard in the relationship. It's scary and painful to let go of what you thought your life was going to be and embark upon the unknown. The more committed you are to your relationship through shared history, marriage, children, and finances, the harder it can be to end it. This is even more the case when there is fear surrounding leaving and when your confidence and self-esteem are at an all-time low after enduring years of systematic emotional mistreatment.

Is This Really Love? will help you ask the right questions to determine whether your relationship is unhealthy. Examining if there is coercion or control in your relationship, two key aspects that are often hard to identify when you are dealing with a highly skilled manipulator, will help you gain clarity about the bigger patterns in your relationship. Additionally, Leah helps you look at your own past experiences, familial history, and possible trauma that, if left unaddressed, can stand in your way of having the healthy partnership you deserve. Learning to slow down and check in with your own body is paramount, as well as observing your own conscious and unconscious thought patterns. *Is This Really Love?* will guide you through all of these steps, acting as your personal road map as you strengthen yourself individually and in your relationship. This important work will serve you in all of your relationships, both current and in the future.

If you determine that your relationship is emotionally abusive, Leah not only walks you through what you can expect when leaving your partner, but she also gives clear instructions on how to navigate these treacherous waters. This expert advice will help you know where to set boundaries with your partner and how to stick to them, giving you the best chance of successfully ending the relationship while preserving integrity on both sides.

I wish you the very best as you embark upon this journey of self-discovery and strength. You are in expert hands with Leah's guidance.

—Avery Neal, PhD, LPC

Introduction

Relationships, by their very nature, are inherently complex. While they can be incredibly meaningful and fulfilling, they can also be challenging and often require a lot of work, including communication, problem solving, and compromise. When two people with their own unique backgrounds, upbringings, and lived experiences merge their lives, it is only natural for conflict, misunderstanding, and difficult situations to arise. In a healthy, mutually respectful, and balanced relationship, these types of challenges (while still very difficult) are generally manageable.

However, when you are in an unhealthy or abusive relationship, sometimes even the most mundane aspects of the relationship can feel like an uphill battle. These types of relationships don't just simply require "work" to sustain but also self-abandonment—neglecting or forgoing your own needs for the sake of your partner. Unfortunately, when a relationship is not explicitly abusive, it can be hard to differentiate the two—"work" from "self-abandonment." In this book, you will come to fully understand the differences between these and recommit to yourself and the life you want and deserve.

• My Story

My emotionally abusive partner picked at me and criticized me for almost everything I did and everything I was. He criticized my food preferences—he hated that I didn't like seafood and would lecture me about this (over and over and over again). He criticized my taste in music. He criticized me for how I cleaned my home (like how I didn't always wring my sponge out completely after doing the dishes). And he criticized me for my hobbies and interests, including my devout viewing of a specific reality television franchise.

He would get annoyed with me anytime I would spill, drop, or bump into something. He regularly expressed judgment of my previous relationships and dating experiences. He was judgmental about some of my friends, my work and career aspirations, and how I chose to spend my free time. While there was a part of me that knew this dynamic was unhealthy, there was also another part of me that had so much empathy and compassion for my partner—the part of me that knew he had past trauma and was hopeful that he would work through these experiences and that things could get better. But it didn't. And then I had my "chicken wing moment."

We were having dinner together. There had been some tension earlier that day, but I tried to push it aside and enjoy our evening. We had grabbed some drinks before and were laughing and having a good time—I finally felt like I could breathe and relax. But, of course, this was short-lived. After finishing our appetizer (chicken wings), he looked at me and asked, "Has anyone ever told you that you lick your fingers when you eat wings?"

He went on to express his concerns about being able to take me to his work events and dinners—worried that I wouldn't be able to conduct myself appropriately in front of his colleagues and that I would embarrass him. It was this moment when everything clicked: Nothing I did would ever be good enough for this person. He would always find a flaw and something to criticize me for. I ended that relationship right then and there and set off to begin my own healing journey.

Through therapy and self-reflection, I was able to recognize just how much this relationship had taken a toll on my mental health and body: I was constantly on edge and anxious. I had regular tension headaches and constipation. I had stopped spending time with certain friends and started to take on the hobbies and interests of this person and neglected the things I had previously enjoyed doing. And I was more self-conscious and worried about my weight and body image. It became evident that despite my efforts to deny the reality of this relationship (telling myself and others things like "He really loves me," "He's a good guy," and "He's working on his issues"), the relationship was costly and harmful to me.

I actively started to do "the work" as we therapists like to call it. I began to work through and challenge some of the negative core beliefs that had been imposed on me. I reengaged in my friendships and other important relationships in my life and spent more time investing in the things that made me feel good about myself and brought me joy. And, eventually, when I jumped back into the dating scene, I approached it with intention and from a place of empowerment. I was clearer than ever about what I wanted and what I knew I deserved.

As a trauma and certified Eye Movement Desensitization and Reprocessing (EMDR) therapist who has spent most of her career supporting individuals in recovering from abusive relationships, as well as someone who has had firsthand experience in an abusive dynamic, I understand how complicated these relationships are and how difficult they can be to leave—especially when the abuse is coercive and controlling. I'm more than familiar with the different and conflicting feelings that often arise: love, confusion, resentment, shame, self-doubt, and fear. I'm also aware of just how impactful these relationships can be on your mental health and sense of self-worth, and the long-term effects that can persist even after you have fully separated yourself from an abusive partner. Most importantly, I know the healing process is never straightforward or linear and that it requires a lot of inner work and courage. This book was designed to reflect this very specific, and sometimes lonely, experience.

Using concepts and interventions from EMDR, acceptance and commitment therapy, motivational interviewing, and self-compassion, this book offers you education, space for reflection, and the skills you need to break old patterns and heal. Think of this book as your loyal, nonjudgmental companion that is going to be there for you as you work through all the muck that comes with navigating and/or breaking free from a coercive, controlling, and emotionally abusive relationship.

In chapter 1, you will come to have a better understanding of what constitutes a healthy relationship and, inversely, what makes a relationship unhealthy or abusive. You will learn about the range of abuse that can occur in a relationship dynamic and gain better insight into the nuanced nature of emotional abuse and how this form of abuse can be difficult to initially see and detect. Chapter 2 will help you understand the emotionally abusive partner—who they are, why they do what they do, the reality of their personality, and their lack of capacity to change.

In chapter 3, you will turn inward and reflect on how you feel or have felt in your relationship. You will consider your sense of safety and emotional well-being, as well as how this relationship might have bled into other areas of your life, such as your work, friendships, and family life. And in chapter 4, you'll work through the cognitive dissonance that occurs when you have been abused by someone you love and care about. Here, I will gently challenge you to confront the fantasy version and potential of this relationship you have been clinging to and accept the reality of the abuse and turmoil it has caused.

Chapter 5 addresses the challenges that naturally come with ending a relationship with an emotionally abusive partner. You will become familiar with some of the hurdles you will most likely encounter, including communication breakdowns; the emotionally abusive partner's pushback, protesting, and emotional distress; the feelings of guilt you might experience; and the boundaries that will be tested. You'll learn about the importance of assertive communication and develop the skills you need to set and reinforce firm boundaries.

In chapter 6, you will learn about the aftereffects of emotional abuse and how this could manifest in your life post abuse. You will understand the role of complex trauma and how, if left unhealed, it can result in changes in the body and mind, including the different types of trauma responses, such as heightened anxiety, self-doubt, mistrust, and low self-esteem. You will also begin to process and reconcile feelings of grief that can surface along with the relief that also comes with leaving. In chapter 7, you will start to fully understand just how deep the emotional abuse can impact you and your core beliefs. And then you will explore and challenge some of your thinking habits and beliefs that are products of the abuse.

In chapter 8, I will invite you to take some time to heal and practice self-compassion. You will be encouraged to hold space for and honor all the feelings that may be arising, including feelings of overwhelm. You will also be asked to dive a little bit deeper and consider how your family of origin, unhealed trauma, and social conditioning may have made you more vulnerable to the emotional abuse you've experienced.

Chapter 9 is all about your self-empowerment and thriving in your future relationships. In this chapter, you will have the opportunity to explore and reconnect with your core values, learn about your relationship rights, and uncover how to shift from a "codependent" mindset to an "interdependent" mindset. This chapter will encourage you to live authentically and create a life that is reflective of who you are and the things that matter to you. Lastly, two reflection exercises included in this book are also available for download at http://www.newharbinger.com/55480.

As you make your way through these chapters, I urge you to be gentle and patient with yourself and try to withhold self-judgment that can (and probably will) come up. You are not alone in this experience—many individuals are afflicted by emotionally abusive relationships.

Remember: You are right where you need to be and you are on track to break free from the abuse.

Chapter 1

The Nuance of Subtle Abuse

Being in an unhealthy or abusive relationship is confusing. Despite the toxicity and distress it causes, there also can be deep feelings of love, commitment, and loyalty. I have a strong feeling that you didn't enter the relationship with the understanding it would be tumultuous or cause you this much pain or emotional duress. Instead, you were most likely drawn to this other person's positive qualities or what they promised you in the beginning stages of the relationship. There was obviously something you saw in this person that was attractive, comforting, familiar, or safe (at least at the time). Or maybe you simply saw their potential and what you thought they "could" be.

All that being said, I know how difficult it can be to come to terms with the reality of an abusive relationship—to even just use the words "abuse" or "abusive" in the same sentence when referring to your relationship or partner/ex-partner can bring up so many different feelings. It's not easy and any aversion you may be experiencing is normal. But having a strong understanding of abuse, what it is, and what it can look like is imperative to your healing and growth.

Throughout this chapter and book, I will be referencing fundamental principles and concepts based on the Duluth Model, which will be explained shortly, and the Equality and Power and Control Wheels (Domestic Abuse Intervention Programs n.d.). The Equality and Power and Control Wheels are graphics that break down the various components of healthy relationships and abusive relationships. It should also be noted that while this model is intentionally gender-specific, it offers universally affirming principles of what it means to be in a healthy relationship. If you are interested in learning more, visit https://www.theduluthmodel.org/wheels/ and https://www.theduluthmodel.org/wheel-gallery/ for more information.

Before we get deep into the trenches of exploring and understanding your personal experiences in an unhealthy or abusive relationship, in this chapter, you will learn what makes a relationship "healthy": the qualities of a healthy relationship, what it looks like, how it should feel, and the green flags to look out for. From here, you will learn more about the nature of abuse and abusive relationships. You will understand the power and control dynamic and the different forms of abuse that can occur. Most importantly, you'll gain a clearer understanding of the nuance of subtle, emotional abuse that can make this type of abuse difficult to detect.

What's "Healthy"?

Most of us learn about relationships from what we experienced and observed during our childhood. If we witnessed abuse or unhealthy dynamics between our parents or caregivers or experienced abuse firsthand, these experiences typically play into our understanding of relationships, shape our expectations of how other people can and/or will treat us, and influence how we navigate our own adult relationships. And even if we did observe a fairly healthy dynamic between our parents or other adults in our immediate environment, most of us were probably never sat down and received an explanation like "This is what a healthy relationship is, why it works, and how you can find one yourself." So, how do you know what's *healthy* if you were never taught or don't have the working knowledge? And how can you even recognize abuse if you don't even know the very basics? You need to know the "green flags" so you can spot the "yellow" and "red flags" (which aren't as easy to detect as we think sometimes). Let's discuss what makes a relationship healthy.

A relationship is healthy when there is mutual trust and respect, stability and consistency, open communication, and shared responsibility. In a healthy relationship, you and your partner are both active participants and have an equal say about the terms of the relationship and the expectations you have for one another—it's a partnership. You are able to express your feelings openly and communicate your needs without fear of judgment or consequences. You can show up exactly as you are and know that you will be accepted for all parts of you. You generally feel at peace because you have trust and faith in your partner and your relationship (Duluth Model).

Below are relationship "green flags" that indicate and reflect a healthy dynamic. As you read through these green flags, consider what feelings come up. Do these green flags feel familiar or foreign? Do they seem obvious or are they surprising? Try to notice what comes up for you, without judgment.

Relationship Green Flags

- Your lines of communication are open and communication is consistent.

- You listen to one another and allow the other person to speak and share their thoughts and perspectives. It feels safe to communicate your feelings, needs, and concerns.

- You work together to resolve conflict and are both open to compromise and finding common ground.

- You both take accountability for your actions and can acknowledge fault. When either of you make a mistake or hurt the other's feelings, you take actionable steps to repair the relationship.

- You respect and value one another in the relationship.

- You are both able to maintain your own identity and autonomy and have a life outside of the relationship.

- You make big decisions together and consider the other person's individual needs when engaging in decision making.

- You both support one another in your personal endeavors and goals.

While no relationship looks exactly the same, these qualities are crucial to sustaining a healthy relationship that is based on equality. Alternatively, in an abusive relationship, there is a lack of equality and, instead, a power-and-control dynamic.

What's "Abuse"?

When you think of the word "abuse" in terms of a romantic relationship, what comes to mind? We tend to think of "abuse" in terms of the extremes—like how it's portrayed in the movies or television. For many, "abuse" is associated with physical assault or when someone is verbally assaulted by their partner—like being cursed at or called derogatory names. We think of the alcoholic husband who comes home drunk and agitated, taking his anger out on his female spouse. We think of the "battered woman" who is isolated and confined to her home. And while abuse can look like the scenarios described above or fall into this category of abuse—domestic violence—there is a range of abuse that can occur within any relationship dynamic.

Abuse can be understood as any act or behavior that asserts power and control over another person and infringes on their rights and autonomy. Abuse varies in type, severity, and frequency. Abuse can be overt or more covert in nature and wax and wane over a period of time. Abuse also occurs in both heterosexual and queer relationships and is not gendered—anyone can be a victim or perpetrator of abuse.

There are three categories of abuse: physical abuse, sexual abuse, and emotional (psychological) abuse.

> **Physical abuse** is any type of nonconsensual, physical assault or act of violence that occurs in a relationship dynamic. This can include throwing objects, hitting, punching, grabbing, pushing, pulling, or choking. Any act that is intended to hurt/physically harm someone is a form of physical abuse.
>
> **Sexual abuse** is any type of sexual aggression that occurs in a relationship dynamic. Sexual abuse includes sexual harassment, coercing someone to engage in sex or other forms of physical intimacy,

rape or forcing any type of sexual contact or touching, and taking or distributing explicit pictures of someone without their consent.

Emotional abuse is any nonphysical act that is intended to inflict emotional pain or diminish a person's self-worth and self-esteem. This form of abuse can be explicit and show up in a relationship as name-calling, yelling, berating, and using public humiliation. It can also be more subtle, which involves controlling behaviors and coercion.

Subtle Abuse

As mentioned above, there is a continuum when it comes to abusive behavior. It can look very different from relationship to relationship—especially in an emotionally abusive dynamic. Emotional abuse can be glaringly obvious—like one partner screaming at the other—and it can also be more subtle, like regular criticism or jokes made at the other's expense. The latter, *subtle abuse*, is typically more difficult to detect and disentangle yourself from because it is so nuanced and often occurs gradually throughout a relationship. Subtle abuse is sneaky because it involves coercion and control.

Coercion

Coercion can be understood as a tactic or "systematic pattern of behavior" that is intended to push or persuade another person into some form of submission or concession—ultimately, it's a means of manipulation (Dichter et al. 2018). Sometimes, coercion includes the use of guilt and shame, making threats, or eliciting empathy. Other times, it may involve appealing to someone's morals and ethos or the use of false promises. Coercion tactics rely on provoking an emotional response. Here are a number of ways manipulation may be used to elicit a specific response from you:

- **Coercion through empathy:** Your partner elicits empathy and compassion by leaning on their past trauma, previous relationships, or mental health challenges to justify unkind or disrespectful behavior and avoid accountability.

Example: *Your partner cheats on you and says, "I didn't want to cheat on you. It's just that I'm insecure and grew up with poor role models and that makes me afraid of commitment."*

- **Coercion through love:** Your partner challenges your love for them or commitment to the relationship to get you to do something you don't want to do or is at odds with your values and expectations for the relationship.

  Example: *Your partner questions your love for them and says, "If you really loved me, you would stay home with me instead of going out with your friends." So, you cancel your plans to prove your love.*

- **Coercion through hope:** Your partner invokes hope by making false promises of change or action to maintain your commitment to them or avoid a breakup.

  Example: *Your partner tells you, "I promise I'm going to change. I'm going to go to therapy!" but either doesn't go or goes only once or twice and then continues to engage in the same behaviors that you have expressed concern about.*

- **Coercion through blame:** Your partner rationalizes their problematic behavior by blaming you, pointing to your past mistakes or flaws as the cause. This use of deflection often fuels self-blame and feelings of shame, which can make it difficult to challenge your partner.

  Example: *When your partner screams at you and then tells you, "If you hadn't been late, I wouldn't have been so angry and yelled."*

- **Coercion through criticism:** Your partner regularly criticizes you or puts you down about things that are seemingly insignificant, so you question yourself and your judgment and defer to them as an authority when making decisions, big and small.

  Example: *Your partner criticizes what you eat and tells you, "Do you really want to eat that? It's so fatty," and this influences your future choices about what you order at a restaurant or eat.*

- **Coercion through authority:** Your partner asserts authority about a specific issue or topic to get you to change your behavior or perspective. They'll say things and make statements with conviction—as if what they say is factual and "true" versus stating an opinion, preference, or personal bias—and you believe them because this is someone you trust.

    Example: *You start questioning your relationship with your parent because of some of the comments your partner has made, such as, "I don't know why you call your mom so much. She's nosy and doesn't respect our privacy."*

Exercise: Pause and Reflect

Take a moment to reflect on your relationship and think about how your partner has used coercion tactics. Consider the timeline of your relationship and when the coercive behaviors started. How did this use of coercion influence your own behavior and make you feel?

Control

Controlling behaviors are actions or efforts made to limit and infringe on another person's autonomy and privacy. Controlling behaviors typically involve imposing one's own beliefs, expectations, and lifestyle onto someone else. Sometimes, they can present as overt—like a demand. Other times, controlling behaviors are more covert and can look like a firm request or suggestion. Below are some of the common methods of control that exist in an emotionally abusive dynamic.

- **Control through isolation:** Your partner isolates you from your support system by telling you who you can and cannot spend time with or trying to limit how much time you spend with certain people.

    Example: *Your partner informs you that you spend "too much time" with your family or close friend and need to focus on the* relationship, so you stop actively making plans with your loved ones.

- **Control through intrusion:** Your partner intrudes on your privacy by requesting to have access to your phone, social media accounts, or other technology to keep tabs on what you are doing outside of the relationship.

    Example: *Your partner demands to read your text messages or look through your call log without any real legitimate reason and makes you feel bad if you push back because that may indicate you are hiding something.*

- **Control through behavior:** Your partner tells you how to do things based on their standards, comfortability, and expectations, like how you should dress or how you should behave in public.

    Example: *Your partner asks you to change what you are wearing to make them more "comfortable," so you adjust or adapt because you care about them and want them to feel seen and heard.*

- **Control through enmeshment:** Your partner pushes to enmesh your lives by sharing resources, such as money, transportation, or even your support system to create dependency, thus making it difficult for you to leave.

    Example: *Your partner insists you share a single car or combine finances earlier on in the relationship despite your discomfort or readiness.*

Exercise: Pause and Reflect

Take a moment to reflect on your relationship and consider the various ways your partner may have tried to control you. When did you first start noticing these controlling behaviors? Did they escalate over time? How did these controlling behaviors impact you?

It's More Than "Work"

The thing about subtle abuse is that it often feels harmless—at least initially. When it is first experienced, it's easy to write it off as being "not that big of a deal." When you care about a person and are committed to the relationship, adjusting or changing your behavior, or doing things slightly differently doesn't seem like that big of an ask or request. And when you trust this person, you're less likely to question their intent or motivation or consider these behaviors as being abusive.

But abuse is rarely a single occurrence, and when it compounds, you can often *feel* the impact—on your health, self-worth, and overall well-being. This is when it becomes harder to simply look the other way or call it "working on a relationship." While compromise and adapting are important and integral in most successful relationships, the work should never be completely one-sided. In a healthy and balanced relationship, it's a partnership. There is a mutual understanding that work is required—but not at the expense of either partner's well-being. You don't work against each other but with each other and equally contribute to the relationship.

Relationship Safety Self-Assessment

Before you dive in and read any further, take a moment to assess the health and safety of your relationship using this self-assessment tool.

1. "I can be myself with my partner without fear." Yes/No
2. "I can express my thoughts and opinions freely with my partner." Yes/No
3. "I am comfortable communicating and expressing my needs to my partner." Yes/ No
4. "I can make mistakes around my partner without judgment." Yes/No
5. "I feel accepted by my partner." Yes/No

6. "I feel seen and heard by my partner." Yes/No
7. "I can change my mind with my partner without consequence." Yes/No
8. "I can set firm boundaries that will be respected by my partner." Yes/No
9. "I can do things independently from my partner." Yes/No
10. "I feel respected by my partner." Yes/No

If you responded no to any of these prompts, this is your sign to turn inward and get curious. While it may feel easier to ignore the yellow or red flags, as you read through the rest of this book, I encourage you to take the time to consider all aspects of your relationship. Focus on your inner experience, how you are feeling, and needs that may be going unmet.

Let's Recap

Confronting an emotionally abusive relationship is difficult. When you don't *really* know what's healthy and the abuse you've endured isn't so blatant, it can make it that much more confusing. It's also hard to face the reality of being in a committed relationship with someone you love or care about that has also cost you so much. However, understanding what *is* and *is not* healthy and familiarizing yourself with the coercion tactics and controlling behaviors you may have been subjected to in your relationship are important in your healing and taking your power back. Next, you will learn about the emotionally abusive partner to gain even more perspective and help you fully see this person—their good and bad parts—and better understand this personality type.

Chapter 2

Understanding the Emotionally Abusive Partner

Emotionally abusive partners (EAP) are difficult to leave because of how complex they are and the regular emotional whiplash that occurs throughout the relationship. One moment, you could be feeling incredibly secure and connected to your partner, and then, just seconds later, you are feeling beaten down and unseen. A client of mine used the word "bamboozled." This term illustrates the inner experience perfectly. It's hard to leave a partner or relationship when it constantly makes you question yourself and your judgment. However, when you can take a step back and understand the personality and patterns of the EAP, it becomes a little bit easier to pull yourself out of the chaos and off the roller coaster.

In this chapter, you will develop a better understanding of the emotionally abusive partner, including their emotional immaturity. You will learn about the role of unresolved trauma in the development of this type of personality. You'll also develop a clearer understanding of the fixed traits and qualities these individuals possess, the patterns of behavior they engage in, and the challenges you typically encounter while being in a relationship with this type of individual. Self-educating and more accurately seeing the relationship with an EAP is imperative for your deprogramming. I promise that it is *not* you—it's them.

Why Are They This Way?

For us to better understand or make sense of the emotionally abusive partner, it's helpful to recognize the role of attachment and trauma in the development of this reactive personality. This person doesn't become abusive overnight and people aren't born with an "abusive" gene. Emotionally abusive patterns typically result from attachment-related trauma that occurs during one's childhood and formative years.

So, what *is* attachment? Attachment is the experience of how we emotionally connect to other people. Attachment theory proposes that how we connect with others and our capacity to navigate our relationships is directly related to our early childhood experiences and how we bonded with our caregivers. To keep it simple: strong and secure attachments to our parents/caregivers predict higher self-esteem and healthier behaviors and relationships in adulthood. However, newer research has indicated that one's attachment style goes beyond these earlier experiences and relationships with our caregivers. This means attachment can also be impacted by peer relationships and other significant relationships throughout our lives (Levine and Heller 2011).

Attachment influences our self-concept and how we see ourselves in relation to others. It influences our ability to trust others, have meaningful relationships, and our general sense of self-worth. When we feel seen, heard, and respected in our close relationships, we tend to do well in our relationships and are capable of emotional intimacy. On the flip side, if we have been abandoned, abused, or neglected by others, we can really struggle, leading to an avoidant, anxious, or disorganized attachment style (which we will discuss further in Chapter 8).

While many of us experience attachment wounds or upsetting experiences that can sometimes cause difficulty and disruption in our relationships, when someone has experienced attachment trauma—a series of experiences in childhood that posed a threat to one's sense of safety and belonging—and has not had sufficient resources and support to heal, the long-term effects can be costly. Emotionally abusive individuals are often the way they are because of unhealed attachment trauma that has resulted in feelings of loneliness, disconnection, victimization, and deep-rooted, negative beliefs about themselves and the world. They typically have high-conflict personalities because they have internalized these past experiences and their persistent fear of rejection and abandonment. This is why they are highly reactive and impulsive, especially in response to stressors that occur in their relationships.

Additionally, research has shown that these types of personalities have a different brain structure and neurobiology compared to those of emotionally mature individuals. Individuals with unresolved attachment trauma have been found to have higher levels of the stress hormone norepinephrine because of overactivity of the amygdala, which is what activates that fight-flight-freeze response (Cozolino 2014). It has also been found that they exhibit greater hippocampal compromise/damage, the part of the brain that is crucial for our "conscious, logical, and cooperative social functioning" (Bernheim et al. 2022). Acknowledging this difference in brain chemistry is significant because it demonstrates that the problematic or concerning behavior we observe in EAPs is typically fixed and the result of how their brain interprets and responds to information.

Personality Traits and Qualities

What's most noticeable about the EAP is that they lack emotional maturity. Their behavior is extreme and unregulated and their reactions are often disproportionate to the situation, which can be incredibly confusing and frustrating to respond to. As you read through the following traits and qualities, consider how they might have shown up in your relationship.

Egocentric

Emotionally abusive partners are egocentric, meaning they are extremely self-involved. Like a child, they are their primary frame of reference. Their needs are more important and more pressing than yours or anyone else's, so their behaviors and decisions are often self-serving, reflecting their needs over the needs of others. Because they are so self-focused, it can feel and read as narcissistic—they are the center of the universe and everything revolves around *them*.

While EAPS are not necessarily completely void of empathy, because they are so caught up in their own inner experience, they have a difficult time putting themselves in other people's shoes or engaging in perspective-taking. This usually results in imbalances in their relationship dynamics because they tend to take up all the space, bring conversations back to them, and don't always have an interest in the lives of others. This is the person who either doesn't ask how you are doing or, if they do, quickly moves on to another subject.

In relationships, this egocentrism can make it difficult for EAPs to truly understand or empathize with the feelings of their partner or make decisions that reflect both their and their partner's needs and interests. They are unrelenting in their views and perspectives—even when presented with reasonable alternatives. It can often feel like they are "in it to win it" and resistant to compromising or meeting in the middle. They like being "right" and see their way as the "right way."

Hypersensitive and Easily Dysregulated

While being sensitive is by no means inherently bad or negative, EAPs are *hypersensitive*. Because they are egocentric and have experienced past mistreatment or abandonment, it's common for them to misinterpret a situation or interaction and take it personally or respond out of fear. They are hypersensitive to the changes in mood, behavior, and perceived stress of others, which then influences their own mood lability. Therefore, their responses to normal environmental stressors can seem dramatic or extreme. For example, they might take someone being playful or making a joke as a personal slight.

Just like a child, emotionally abusive partners are reactive and struggle with effectively regulating their emotions. They have a difficult time being able to identify and understand their reactions, self-soothe, and express their feelings to others in a mature and appropriate way. Subsequently, they have regular outbursts that can look a lot like tantrums. They might also pout, shut down, or leave a situation due to poor impulse control.

In relationships, EAPs can come off as very "hot and cold." One moment, they are pleasant and warm—the next, they are angry or reactive. They often switch from being very loving and adoring of their partner to agitated and resentful. When you are in a relationship with an EAP, it often feels as though you are having to constantly walk on eggshells, which can make it difficult to freely speak and express yourself.

Emotional Reasoning and Lack of Cognitive Flexibility

EAPs often lack the ability to think critically because "the intense emotions and anxiety that emotionally immature people experience can decrease their ability to think at this higher level" (Gibson 2015). Instead of using logic, they tend to default to emotional reasoning: their thoughts reflect how they are *feeling* in the moment. This emotional reasoning limits their capacity to think conceptually and reason appropriately—which can make it difficult to have productive conversations.

Similar to children, emotionally abusive partners are typically rigid and inflexible in their thinking, seeing things as "black and white," "good and bad," and "right and wrong." They tend to think concretely and respond to what's in front of them versus thinking in the abstract, making it difficult for them to problem solve or think in terms of "gray." They have a difficult time seeing outside of themselves and their fixed ideas and interpretations of the world. If something doesn't fit or complement their worldview, they are often resistant and unwilling to consider alternative ideas or perspectives.

In relationships, you will often find yourself talking in circles, trying to rationalize or reason with an EAP. Arguments are challenging and often go unresolved because of their lack of cognitive flexibility.

Limited Self-Awareness

Emotionally abusive partners have limited self-awareness: they are not very self-reflective or aware of how their actions impact others or are perceived by others. They have a difficult time being able to recognize their problematic behaviors and therefore do not usually feel motivated to change their behavior. They might go to therapy or seek support when they are experiencing emotional distress, but they tend to fixate on the behaviors of others versus their own.

This limited self-awareness can also manifest in an inaccurate self-image. While most of us cannot be completely objective in how we view or see ourselves, EAPs *really* struggle with objectivity because of their limited self-awareness. Their perception of themselves can be pretty skewed and contradict what other people around them observe. For example, an EAP might present as highly anxious to others (i.e., they bite their nails, are restless, and regularly express worry), but see themselves as being cool, calm, and collected. Another example is an EAP claiming to be "thoughtful" or "generous," but typically doesn't go out of their way to make other people comfortable or do things not strictly out of obligation.

In relationships, these partners struggle with accountability and being able to see how their behaviors can be hurtful or damaging. They tend to have a difficult time recognizing their part in a conflict and assuming responsibility. This quality hinders them from making real and lasting changes or seeing the need for personal growth to improve the state of the relationship.

Need for Control

Due to previous experiences that made them feel unsafe or helpless, EAPs often prefer order and predictability because they offer them a sense of safety and control. They can come across as neurotic with very specific preferences and needs that don't always make sense and tend to try to impose these preferences and needs onto others. They prefer things to be done in a way that feels good and safe for them—even if it is at the expense of others or makes other people uncomfortable.

This need for control can manifest in a variety of ways, including needing to be in charge of plans, dominating conversations, and obsessing over order and cleanliness. They also see their friends, family, and partners as an extension of themselves and can become upset or frustrated when the people closest to them express opposing feelings or beliefs. They can be pushy and try to impose their opinions onto others while making no or little attempt to gain an understanding of alternative opinions. When they feel out of control, they will often have a tantrum or protest to communicate their distress and discomfort.

In relationships, the emotionally abusive partner's need for control often manifests in a variety of controlling behaviors (both consciously and unconsciously) that infringe on the autonomy of their partner. They tend to hold the belief that they have a say in what their partner does, who they spend time with, their interests, and their values. They will also try to dictate the terms of the relationship and set expectations that feel unreasonable or unattainable.

Attention-Seeking

Because of their attachment wounds and challenges with their self-esteem and sense of self-worth, attention is so meaningful. They want to feel loved and important and, therefore, seek out people, situations, and relationships that are affirming. They also tend to engage in attention-seeking behaviors—specific behaviors that will result in either positive or negative attention. Whether it's them sighing loudly, slamming a door to provoke concern from others, or being loud and gregarious at a work holiday party—they want to be seen, heard, and responded to.

In relationships, these attention-seeking behaviors can show up in different ways. They might make a grand or dramatic gesture to win you over after a fight or try to charm the people in your life who matter most to you as a means of seeking their approval. When they are feeling upset, they will engage in behaviors that draw attention and evoke empathy and support from their partner.

Emotional Immaturity Does Not Excuse Abuse

Emotionally abusive partners are not inherently "bad" or "evil." They are who they are because of complex trauma that has influenced how they think, feel, and behave. And while it's important to acknowledge the role of trauma and attachment in the personality development of these individuals, this doesn't excuse abuse or unkind behavior. Regardless of their past or lack of emotional maturity, EAPs still need to be held accountable and you have the right to be free from the manipulation and trauma caused by the relationship.

Exercise: Pause and Reflect

Take a moment to consider your relationship. Would you allow anyone else to treat you this way? Would you treat others the same way your partner has treated you? If the answer is no, make a mental note of this and regularly remind yourself that you, just like everyone else, deserve to be treated with kindness, respect, and consideration.

Let's Recap

Relationships with emotionally abusive partners are both emotionally taxing and perplexing. Familiarizing yourself with the personality traits and qualities of the EAP and the role of attachment and trauma can help you gain perspective and have more realistic expectations. While it's understandable for you to have compassion for this person whom you love and/or care for, it's also imperative that there is accountability and that the EAP is held to the same standards that you have for yourself and others. In chapter five, you will learn more about the importance of accountability, including how to end a relationship with an EAP, as well as set limits and firm boundaries with this person who has been abusive toward you. But next, we will focus on validating what it has felt like being in a relationship with an emotionally abusive partner.

Chapter 3

How It Feels to Be in a Relationship with an Emotionally Abusive Partner

Knowing what's abusive and being able to understand the complexity of the emotionally abusive partner and their patterns of behavior is one thing. Being able to detect abuse in your relationship is another. Even if you have working knowledge of what makes a relationship "healthy" versus "unhealthy," it's also possible you may be vulnerable to your own blind spots. It's hard to be completely objective in our relationships. When we are in the thick of it, we don't have the distance and perspective we might have if we were evaluating someone else's relationship, like a family member's or a close friend's. We only have what's right there in front of us—which, of course, is in many ways influenced by our partner and other external factors we aren't always consciously aware of.

In this chapter, you're going to be turning inward. First, you will be asked to turn down the noise—identify and create distance from some of those outside influences and distractions that may be preventing you from connecting with how you are feeling. Next, you will be asked to shift your focus to your inner experience as it relates to your relationship. You will focus on how you *feel* in your relationship and with your partner without all the noise of those outside influences. You will also explore how this relationship may be bleeding into or impacting other areas of your life.

I recognize that this phase of your healing can be overwhelming, especially given the conflicting feelings that naturally arise when confronting the reality of an unhealthy or abusive relationship. Remember, it's important to continue to maintain curiosity and an open mind. The purpose is not to judge but for you to bring more awareness to this inner experience and consider how this relationship could be negatively impacting your mental health and overall well-being.

Tuning Out the Noise

It can be difficult to tune in to how we are *really* feeling when we are easily distracted and swayed by our environment and other outside influences. This noise can make it difficult for us to slow down and pay close attention to our inner experience and what our body is communicating to us. It can make us question ourselves and second-guess our intuition or judgment. Part of tuning in to how we are feeling requires tuning out this noise. Below are some of the outside influences that can compromise this inner knowing that something just isn't quite right.

Partner Influence

When you are in an emotionally abusive relationship, you are heavily influenced by your partner—their experiences, perceptions, and biases. This includes their personal beliefs, values, and worldview, as well as the expectations they have for the relationship and you as their partner. This also may include how they understand the relationship dynamic and make sense of their abusive behaviors. For example, your partner may hold the belief that their abusive behavior is justified because they are simply responding from a place of anger and do not have any control over how they react. Another example is an abusive partner attributing a specific behavior (like jealousy or possessiveness) to their gender. These rationalizations can sometimes cause you to second-guess your own reality and experience as the person who is being abused.

Your experience is also likely to be influenced by the love and compassion you have for your partner. As discussed in chapter 2, there is a high likelihood that your partner's behavior is an outcome of past experiences and trauma or a by-product of mental health challenges or illness. Having this insight and knowing your partner's history can sometimes cloud your ability to take your own needs into account because of the empathy and affection you have for this person whom you see as having been wounded or a victim themselves. You may also be protective of this person and have a sense of loyalty and responsibility to care for them. All of this is understandable and human—recognizing where this is coming from without judgment will be crucial moving forward.

Social Norms and Pressures

Social norms are the "expectations of behavior that you may have been socialized or conditioned to believe as being true" (National Academies of Sciences, Engineering and Medicine et al. 2018). These perceived truths can be imposed on you and perpetuated through media, religion, and the communities you are part of. For example, if you were raised to believe "boys will be boys," this belief may have legitimized the abusive behavior of your male partner. While most of us would like to think that we are immune to the influence of these social norms, social norms have been found to contribute to the normalization of abuse, intimate partner violence, and gender inequality (National Academies of Sciences, Engineering, and Medicine et al. 2018).

Additionally, research has shown that we are largely influenced by the perceived pressure of our social network (family, friends, and peers) to seek out and stay in romantic relationships. This pressure from our social network can create stress and reinforce a fear of being single, which can ultimately make it that much more difficult to leave a relationship that is unhealthy or unsafe (Sprecher and Felmlee 2021).

Family Influence

You can be influenced by your family members' perspectives and biases, including their understanding of relationships and what is "okay" or "normal." This can include what you observed firsthand during childhood or what was directly communicated to you by your parents, caregivers, or other adults in your environment. For example, if your parents had a strained or volatile relationship, abusive behaviors could feel normal or you might see your relationship as being "not that bad" by comparison.

Family noise may also include generational trauma (the trauma that was experienced by generations before you) and some of the negative core beliefs that have been passed down or imposed onto you by your family. Examples of negative core beliefs you might have come to internalize include: "All men are cheaters," "I'm powerless," "I'm not in control," "I can't get what I want," or "I can't trust anyone." These beliefs can play into how you perceive or respond to your relationship and the problematic behaviors of your partner.

Feedback from Others

Additionally, you might be influenced by the feedback you receive from your loved ones about your partner and/or relationship. I've worked with many individuals who have had a difficult time leaving an unhealthy relationship because of how loved their partner was by their family or friends. When the people closest to you have expressed a fondness for your partner or admiration for your relationship, this feedback can create confusion and cause you to doubt your judgment. And, if your partner is charming or charismatic (a common personality trait or quality of EAPs that was discussed in chapter 2), positive feedback about them can be quite common. If everyone around you is telling you how great or wonderful your partner is or they are highly regarded or respected by others, this outside noise can really mess with your head.

Exercise: Pause and Reflect

Before turning inward and focusing on your inner experience, give yourself a moment to take an inventory of any outside influences that could be distracting you or blocking you from connecting with how you are feeling. Consider any of the fears you might have, the social pressures or expectations that might be present, or feedback you have received from others.

Journal prompt: What might be getting in the way of you connecting with how you are feeling or accepting how you are feeling about your partner and relationship?

• Cecelia's Story

Cecelia had initiated therapy because she wanted to feel more secure in her current relationship. She had shared that she had been in an unhealthy relationship in the past and was worried that she was projecting her experiences from her past relationship onto her current partner. She started therapy with the goal of changing her mindset and having more realistic expectations for this new partner. After a few sessions, it became more and more evident that Cecelia was feeling on edge because she wasn't feeling safe in her current relationship. When she would try to broach a more sensitive topic, such as wanting to have more regular communication with her partner while he was traveling for work, he would regularly lash out and call her "crazy" or "immature."

During one session, after a specific blowup, Cecelia was asked, "How do you feel when you are with him?" She paused and gave a thoughtful response. "I feel anxious." She explained that she was always worrying about how her partner might respond to her. As a result, she had started to avoid all sensitive topics or things that might cause her partner to have a negative reaction. She didn't want to upset him or to be invalidated. She came to realize that she was in a relationship dynamic that was harmful to her and her mental health.

How Do You Feel?

Now that you are more aware of some of the potential influences, how do you feel in this relationship? Do you feel at peace or stressed? Do you feel present or disconnected? Do you feel safe? Or do you feel nervous or fearful? And if you have a difficult time identifying a specific emotion, how does your body feel? Focus on the physical sensations you may experience when you are around your partner or when you think about the relationship. For example, maybe you notice your body becoming more tense or that your heart races. These sensations can be informative and signal that something may be off.

It is also possible to experience more than one emotion at any given time or have different emotions that might seem conflicting. Things are rarely straightforward when it comes to relationships—especially when there is subtle abuse present or the relationship has some toxic qualities. Below are different scenarios to consider when turning inward and reflecting on your relationship and how it makes you feel. Read through each of these scenarios and take note of what comes up for you.

1. **Spending quality time with your partner:** How does it feel when you are spending one-on-one time with your partner? How does it feel to share a space with your partner or when you are in their physical presence?

2. **Navigating conflict with your partner:** How does it feel when there is conflict between you and your partner? How does it feel when there is an argument or disagreement?

3. **Expressing your needs to your partner:** How does it feel when you are communicating your needs to your partner? How does it feel when you are asking for something from your partner?

4. **Expressing your feelings to your partner:** How does it feel when you express your feelings to your partner? How does it feel when you are trying to explain your perspective?

5. **Being away from your partner:** How does it feel when you are away from your partner? How does it feel when you are not in contact or communication?

6. **Discussing sensitive topics with your partner:** How does it feel when you and your partner are discussing sensitive topics? How does it feel to initiate a conversation about something that is potentially touchy for your partner?

7. **Being around family and friends with your partner:** How does it feel when you and your partner are in the presence of family? How does it feel when you are out socializing with your partner?

The thing about abusive relationships is that they usually aren't *always* bad and the abusive partner isn't *always* abusive. There are probably many good moments or moments when you feel (or have felt) comfortable or close to your partner. These are the moments that can make it difficult to confront the abuse or even provide justification for the abuse—because there is *some* good. This is why it can be helpful to reflect on and consider all facets of the relationship—to bring awareness to how the relationship impacts you, how it can be a source of comfort—and also, a source of stress.

Exercise: Pause and Reflect

Take some time to consider how you feel in your relationship or how the relationship affects you emotionally. Do you feel mostly good or mostly bad? Are you generally comfortable or do you tend to feel on edge?

Journal prompt: How do you feel in your relationship and in the presence of your partner?

• Bernadette's Story

Bernadette was married to her husband for over ten years and had come to therapy because she was questioning the health of her marriage. "He's a good dad," she had shared in therapy, shortly after describing the verbal abuse she endured from him over the course of the relationship. She was on the fence about whether she should leave him—especially because she was "fine," "had a good life," and shared two young children with him.

Over time, through therapy, it became quite evident that things weren't really "fine." She was experiencing physical health symptoms that her medical providers were unable to diagnose. She was constantly tired, had low energy, and when overwhelmed, would have fainting spells. At one point, she even had to take some time off work due to these persistent health issues.

What's Going on in Your Body?

Sometimes, it can be hard to tap into our emotions. In emotionally abusive relationships, it's common to avoid the reality of the relationship—and this can involve detaching ourselves emotionally (we will discuss this at greater length in chapter 4). While emotional detachment can be helpful in the short term by protecting us from further distress or emotional turmoil or being forced to face the hard decision of ending a relationship, it can also be harmful in the long term because it can keep us in situations and relationships that are detrimental to us. However, even when we are able to emotionally detach, our bodies tend to take on the stress and trauma of the relationship.

When we are experiencing crisis or are in high-stress situations, our sympathetic nervous system is activated, which jump-starts our body's "fight/flight/freeze" response. Activity in the amygdala or "smoke detector" part of our brain results in the release of stress hormones, including cortisol and adrenaline. These hormones are responsible for the "whole body response," which includes increased heart rate, breathing rate, and blood pressure (van der Kolk 2014). And how we recover or stabilize can vary depending on the stressor.

Some stressors we endure are brief and occur as a single incident; other stressors can be chronic and persistent. When a stressor is chronic or persistent and we do not have the opportunity to recover, our bodies respond accordingly and maintain this highly activated state. In this state, we have elevated levels of stress hormones. While these hormones are (by design) adaptive in many ways—by helping us respond quickly to threats and protect ourselves from danger—they can also compromise our physical health. These hormones can weaken our immune system and cause high blood pressure and other ailments, such as digestive problems and chronic pain. Basically, our bodies are directly impacted by stress and can take a huge hit, even when we feel seemingly fine (Sharpley 2009).

Emotionally abusive relationships are inherently stressful. Even if you have learned how to emotionally detach and have become accustomed to the hurtful or problematic behavior of your partner, this chronic stress can manifest in your physical health. Below are some of the common physical health symptoms you may experience while enduring an emotionally abusive relationship. Read through this list of somatic symptoms and consider how your *body* may be responding to the stress of your relationship.

- chronic fatigue
- chronic headaches
- digestive issues
- significant change in appetite
- weight loss
- high blood pressure
- muscle tension
- back pain
- regularly sick/ill
- inconsistent or irregular periods
- loss of hair
- insomnia

Remember, everyone responds to stress differently, but you know your body better than anyone. If you are noticing changes in your body or its functioning—pay attention to it. Our bodies can tell us when we are and aren't doing well—especially if we aren't able to connect to our emotions and how we are feeling mentally.

Exercise: Pause and Reflect

Take some time to connect with your body and how you are feeling physically. Have you noticed any changes in your physical health or any persistent physical symptoms? If so, consider when these changes started and if you have noticed a pattern in these symptoms (i.e., when they are most present or noticeable).

Journal exercise: Keep a daily log of your physical symptoms. In this log, note the symptoms you are experiencing (i.e., tension headache) and what was going on that day (i.e., stressors).

How Are You Functioning?

Another aspect to consider when engaging in self-reflection and assessing the health and state of your relationship is how you are functioning on a more global level. Relationships don't exist in a vacuum; when things are not going well or the dynamic is unhealthy or abusive, the relationship tends to impact your general functioning and bleed into the other areas of your life. Below are examples of how your relationship may be negatively impacting your career or work life, general lifestyle, and personal relationships or social life.

Work-Related Challenges

When we are struggling at home or in our personal life, our work life and career can take a hit. Even if you are *really* good at compartmentalizing, you're human. When you're going through a life crisis or experiencing chronic stress, it's impossible to leave it all at home. When all your time, energy, and emotions are being spent trying to manage and cope with your relationship, it can be hard to maintain your other responsibilities and relationships—which of course includes your work functioning.

Here are some signs that your work and/or job performance might be compromised by your relationship stress:

- Regularly arriving to work late and/or leaving early; increase in absences
- Constantly tired and fatigued
- Lack of focus and concentration; challenges completing tasks or work that was previously manageable
- Decrease in work productivity
- Decrease in motivation or being less invested in your work than usual
- Shorter tempered and irritable toward coworkers
- Reacting emotionally or overreacting to workplace stressors
- Increase in feelings of insecurities around your role and job responsibilities
- Compulsively checking your phone or communicating with your partner during work hours
- Peers/coworkers expressing concerns about you and your wellbeing

These are just a few examples of ways your work functioning can be impacted by the stress of your relationship. Take a moment and consider your work life. Have there been any changes in your performance? Do you feel like you have been more distracted? What about less productive? Even if you are not consciously thinking about the relationship, it may be compromising your ability to optimally function at work or to work at the best of your ability.

• MJ's Story

MJ had sought out therapy because they were having a difficult time in their marriage. Their relationship with their spouse had been a series of ups and downs and they wanted more guidance to help them navigate their relationship. When they were asked how their marriage impacted their day-to-day functioning, MJ's initial response was, "It doesn't really." They explained that they were doing well at work: in fact, they were excelling and had recently been promoted. However, upon further contemplation, they recognized that when they and their partner were at odds, they would drink more—and excessively. They also shared they had stopped regularly running and exercising—an outlet that had always been helpful and effective in managing their stress and maintaining their mental and physical health. They explained that their relationship was draining and that they had very little energy to do anything outside of work and their relationship.

Lifestyle Changes

Another indicator that tells us we may be struggling in our relationship is changes in our lifestyle. Sometimes, how we are coping (or not coping) can clue us in to how we are feeling or doing. Again, when a relationship has depleted you of all your energy, it's common to feel fatigued and unmotivated to do the things that typically bring you joy or engage in those healthy habits that are imperative for your mental, physical, and general well-being.

Additionally, when you are in an abusive dynamic, it is common to engage in unhealthy or harmful coping strategies, such as substance misuse or abuse, to numb yourself and cope with the stress of the relationship.

Here are a few examples of lifestyle changes that can occur:

- Having two or three glasses of wine at home every evening (when typically you only drink on special occasions)
- Changing what you wear and how you dress to reflect your partner's preferences

- Becoming obsessive about what you eat and counting calories because your partner has been commenting on your weight and what you eat

- Going to bed early and sleeping excessively to avoid interacting with your partner

- Not calling back your friends and regularly canceling plans to avoid conflict with your partner

Without judgment, take some time to reflect on and assess your current lifestyle and day-to-day functioning. Have there been any significant changes? Are there things you have been neglecting as a result of your relationship? How are you coping with the stress of your relationship? Are there any new habits that are unhealthy or harmful that you have taken on?

Shifts in Relationships

Oftentimes in emotionally abusive relationships, the other people and relationships in our lives become collateral damage. When your partner is controlling or overly involved, it can be difficult to maintain or sustain the other relationships you have in your life. Whether it's because your partner has expressed feelings of dislike toward a specific person or relationship, they are jealous and possessive, or the abuse has worn you down to the point that you are unable to nurture the other connections in your life, your relationships tend to change or shift—and usually not for the better. It's also normal for individuals in abusive relationships to isolate and avoid friends and loved ones because they don't want to have to talk about or explain their relationship.

Below are some of the ways your relationships and social life may be impacted by your romantic relationship:

- Having less contact with friends and family

- Lacking the desire to socialize or connect with friends and loved ones

- Feeling pressured to involve your partner in your other relationships
- Withholding information from the people you typically are open with
- Feeling more disconnected from the other significant people in your life

Exercise: Pause and Reflect

Consider how your relationship has impacted your life as a whole. Has your life changed for the better or has it gotten worse? What is indicating to you that it has gone in either direction?

Journal exercise: For each life domain (work, lifestyle, social), on its own page, list all the changes or shifts that have occurred since you entered this relationship.

Example: *Work: I feel less focused, I stopped having lunch with my coworkers, I stopped caring about the promotion. Lifestyle: I stopped exercising, I care less about my appearance. Social: I haven't seen my best friend in months.*

Let's Recap

Abuse isn't always blatantly obvious—especially when the abuse is more subtle and you are being influenced by various factors. It's also common to question yourself and rationalize aspects of your relationship that may be problematic. However, when you give yourself the time and space to self-reflect and focus on your inner experience—tuning out all of the noise—you better position yourself to see the relationship more accurately. Take a breath, give yourself a hug, and remember that you are worthy of focusing on yourself. In the next chapter, you will learn a little bit more about yourself and the psychological defenses that may be at play and keeping you in the abusive dynamic.

Chapter 4

Escaping the Fantasy and Acknowledging the Reality

Even when you become fully aware of the toxicity of your relationship and can acknowledge the abusive tendencies of your partner, there may still be a part of you that is hopeful and not ready to end or leave the relationship. When things aren't simply black and white or there are layers to a person or relationship, it's normal to have conflicting feelings and to feel pulled in different directions. You may be thinking, "Yes, my partner can be abusive, but they can also be loving and kind" or "I know they have been hurtful, but my partner isn't a bad person." It can be hard to make sense of or come to peace with the duality (that two seemingly different things can coexist) of emotionally abusive relationships and the reality that the emotionally abusive partner is unlikely to change.

In this next chapter, I will talk about some of the ways you may have been living in a fantasy version of your relationship and how this defense mechanism may be impairing your judgment and ability to make decisions that are in your best interest. You'll learn about the cognitive dissonance that you may be experiencing in your relationship and why it's important to really lean into it and explore what this uncomfortable feeling state may be signaling or communicating to you. Finally, you will be encouraged to face the reality and consider some of the costs of staying in a relationship that is toxic or abusive.

Are You Living in Fantasy Land?

When we are in high-stress situations or in the midst of trauma, we get creative in how we cope—although this typically occurs outside of our consciousness. We have evolved as a species to do fancy mind-footwork: our mind creates a story or narrative to make sense of the things in our lives we can't fully understand or situations that cause us pain. This is done as a form of survival and is your body doing what it was meant to do. When we are in an unhealthy or abusive relationship dynamic, a common defense mechanism is denial. Oftentimes, this denial involves creating a false reality or fantasy version of the relationship—a version that, in the long term, may be keeping you hostage in a harmful situation.

Clinging to the Old Version

- ### Alana's Story

  Alana had been in her relationship for just over two years. When they had first met, her boyfriend was all in. He was romantic and very affirming. He quickly introduced her to his friends and family and was excited to meet and get to know her family and friends. He was thoughtful and would do so many little things to make her feel special, like sharing a song that reminded him of her or posting a picture of them on social media with a sweet and personal caption expressing his love and adoration for her.

  About a year into their relationship, shortly after moving in together, Alana's boyfriend started to become more distant and disengaged. He was less enthusiastic about spending time with her and prioritized his work and spending time with his friends. When Alana would ask to spend more time with him, he would call her "needy." He also started demanding that she take responsibility for all of the household tasks and then criticize how she would clean and cook. She rarely felt appreciated and valued and started to even fear him.

> *Despite these changes in her relationship and the concerns she had about her boyfriend's behavior, she was struggling with the idea of ending the relationship. She was regularly replaying their entire relationship in her head and fixated on the first few months of their relationship. It was hard for her to consider moving on knowing just how wonderful her boyfriend had been when they initially started dating.*

There is a reason you fell for your partner. There was something there—at least one or two qualities—that attracted you to them. Maybe it was the confidence they conveyed, their ambition, or their charismatic nature. Maybe they wore their heart on their sleeve and made you feel incredibly loved or special. Maybe they were looking for the exact same thing you were looking for relationship-wise and expressed similar wants and desires. Whatever the reason, there had to be something that drew you to them. Now, this emotionally abusive partner probably doesn't seem like the same person you fell for—and this is a tough reality to face.

When you know that your partner has the ability to be kind, thoughtful, loving, and respectful, it can be hard to let go of this version of them. You saw the good in them, their shiny qualities, and how they were able to show up for you when they were on their best behavior. Having this firsthand experience and knowing how things *used to be* can create a false sense of hope and faith in this person and relationship. So, instead of accepting the reality, you might cling to this old version of your partner and wait for them to morph back into the person you were initially attracted to. Is it possible that you are getting hung up on the past? Here are some signs that suggest you may be clinging to this past version of your partner:

- You regularly think about how things *were* when you first met this person and reminisce about the past.

- You fantasize about the past version of your partner—focusing on the qualities you loved most about them. You seek out moments and interactions that confirm that your partner still has these qualities—even if they are few and far between.

- When you talk to others about your partner and relationship, you focus solely on the past.

Clinging to the Potential

• Gina's Story

Gina and her boyfriend had a volatile relationship. It had been consistently up and down since the onset of them dating, especially because there had been some dishonesty during the first few months of them seeing each other. Gina's boyfriend hadn't been honest about him dating other people and was still maintaining contact with one of the women he had been seeing prior to him and Gina becoming serious. Additionally, Gina's boyfriend had "anger issues" and had a difficult time managing his anger. When Gina and her boyfriend would argue, he would regularly yell and say hurtful things. While he would apologize and take accountability for these outbursts, they didn't subside and her boyfriend didn't make any real effort to change or do things differently. Gina started to fear arguments and conflict with her boyfriend because of how quickly they would escalate.

Eventually, through lots of persuading, Gina was able to get her partner to agree to couples therapy. But therapy wasn't very effective. Gina's partner was mostly quiet and regularly expressed that he didn't believe therapy would be helpful. Gina didn't know what to do. She knew her partner had a lot of potential. She saw how he was excelling at work and knew how smart and capable he was. She also knew he had experienced a lot of childhood trauma and his anger was most likely related to his past. "If he would just go to therapy," she would tell herself, "things could be so much better." She was clinging to the hope that her partner would get the help he needed and change.

You could be getting caught up in your partner's potential—their capacity to change, grow, and do things differently. This is a common experience for individuals navigating a relationship with an emotionally abusive partner. When you are someone with insight and self-awareness and are motivated to better yourself (which we both *know* you are because you are reading this book), it's reasonable for you to assume that others also share this same growth mindset—a desire to do better and become better versions of themselves. Additionally, if your partner has expressed feelings of regret or remorse for their abusive tendencies, shown some level of insight regarding their behavior being problematic, or promised that they will change or do better, this can further reinforce any hope you might have.

There's also the possibility that your partner has made *some* effort to address their abusive tendencies and change. Maybe they found a therapist and have been to a session or two or have agreed to couples counseling. Maybe they have been on their best behavior for a few days or have made some thoughtful or grand gestures (like buying you gifts or taking you out for a nice meal), which is also known as *love bombing*. When you see this effort being made—even if it's fleeting—you start to feel more optimistic. You tell yourself, "See, they *are* changing."

Take a moment to consider if you have been staying in the relationship because of your partner's potential. Below are some signs that suggest you could be clinging to this potential version:

- When your partner does something hurtful or abusive, you redirect your thoughts to some of the "nice" things your partner has done and the good qualities they have.

- You tend to make excuses for your partner's abusive behavior by attributing it to their past trauma or mental health challenges that they have shared with you.

- You fantasize about how much better things will be when your partner goes to therapy or seeks outside support.

Clinging to the Romanticized

- ### Luke's Story

    Luke was engaged to his partner and their wedding date was set for a few months out. Luke and his partner had a whirlwind romance. They immediately fell hard for one another, quickly moved in together, and were engaged shortly after. Luke had never felt this strongly about anyone before—their relationship was intense. As their wedding approached, Luke started to have some feelings of doubt. His partner was extremely jealous and had a difficult time with him having a social life outside of their relationship; Luke was regularly accused of cheating and flirting. So, to prevent any conflict, Luke was spending less time with his friends and started to avoid social gatherings.

    Luke was feeling conflicted. He and his partner had amazing chemistry and were deeply in love. But he was also beginning to feel worn down and a little lost. When he would start to question the relationship or even just briefly acknowledge some of his feelings of unhappiness, he would try to talk himself out of these thoughts. He would rationalize the relationship by painting it as passionate and intense. He would tell himself that his partner just "loved hard."

There's a possibility that you are clinging to a romanticized version of your relationship because of the "fairy-tale narrative" you have internalized. Through pop culture, we have been socialized to believe that passionate love is inherently volatile and full of ups and downs. Most of the love stories and fairy tales we are intimately familiar with involve high conflict and high stress—think *The Notebook*, *Romeo & Juliet*, or *Titanic*. As a result, many people stay in unhealthy or abusive relationships because they have come to glamorize the toxicity of their relationship. When you value intensity, abusive behaviors might not seem *that* bad despite the hurt or pain they cause.

If you subscribe to this fairy-tale narrative, you are more likely to tolerate certain behaviors. For example, if your partner expresses strong feelings of jealousy or possessiveness, you might find this quality endearing or rationalize it as being a symptom of their deep love for you. If your partner yells at you, you might be more inclined to see it as an act of passion. And if you hold the belief that love will and can conquer all, you might be that much more determined to stay and endure the abuse of the relationship. Is it possible you have been wearing rose-colored glasses and romanticizing your relationship? Here are some signs that suggest you may be getting caught up in this romanticized version of your relationship:

- You are constantly looking toward the future and daydreaming—fantasizing about how your relationship *will* be once things get better.

- You fixate on future relationship milestones, like marriage or starting a family, versus addressing what is going on in the present.

- You try to talk yourself out of any bad feelings you might be having toward your partner and relationship by telling yourself that your partner is reacting out of their love for you.

Exercise: Pause and Reflect

Take some time to consider these three fantasies—clinging to the old version, potential, and romanticized. Get curious and consider how your current or past relationships may have been reflected in these descriptors. Take a moment to think about how this defense mechanism may have helped or harmed you—or both. And then offer yourself some compassion and remind yourself that you're strong and capable of healing from these experiences.

Journal prompt: Identify and write down three to five affirmations that are loving and compassionate. Repeat these affirmations to yourself whenever you start to notice any feelings of shame arise. Remember, you are human and learning from these experiences and deserve the same love and compassion you give to others.

Leaning into Discomfort and Exploring Cognitive Dissonance

When you're in a relationship that is causing you pain and suffering but you are also feeling ambivalent about leaving, this typically results in cognitive dissonance. *Cognitive dissonance* is that uncomfortable feeling you experience when you hold opposing thoughts or feelings about a situation. Oftentimes this occurs when you are acting or behaving in a way that is at odds with your core beliefs and values. This discomfort, while unpleasant, can be incredibly useful. Think of cognitive dissonance as your body informing you, "Hey, something doesn't seem right. Are you sure about this?" I have a strong feeling that being in an emotionally abusive relationship is probably causing you discomfort because it clashes with your values and what you know (at least, deep down) you deserve in a relationship. There is a part of you that knows this relationship is unhealthy and harmful to you.

If you are experiencing cognitive dissonance in your relationship, I encourage you to lean into the discomfort, pause, and check in with yourself. Ask yourself the following questions:

1. What's causing me to feel uncomfortable or uneasy?

2. Is this relationship at odds with my core values and the qualities of a safe and healthy relationship?

3. What are my options? What can I do to address and reduce this discomfort?

Addressing this cognitive dissonance is hard, especially if you have become accustomed to detaching or avoiding difficult thoughts and feelings (which, as you now know from chapter 2, is a common response to emotionally abusive relationships). But it is imperative if you want to escape the fantasy version you have been living in and confront the reality of your emotionally abusive relationship.

Reality Checking

The rest of this chapter is going to focus on challenging this fantasy version of the relationship you might still be clinging to. I will be asking you to really inspect your relationship: look at it with more objectivity, as if you were a scientist, a curious, outside observer. I will also be asking you to confront some of the unrealistic expectations you might have of both you and your partner. Finally, you'll consider the costs of the relationship—the things you might have lost or sacrificed for this emotionally abusive partner.

If There's a Pattern, There's a Problem

Take a moment to step back and consider the EAP's behavior from a place of curiosity. Is there a noticeable pattern in their behavior? Meaning, has there been more than one or two occurrences of abuse? I'm guessing so. Even if there is a period of peace or "good behavior" (behavior that is kind and respectful) in the relationship, the abuse is probably recurring and part of a cycle. In some relationships, the abuse cycle might be rapid: the abusive behavior occurs frequently between brief moments of calm. In others, the instances of abuse might be more spread out. There could be days, weeks, or even months of peace between an outburst (i.e., being screamed or cursed at) or a period of prolonged abuse (i.e., your partner giving you the silent treatment for an extended period of time, or your partner criticizing you on a daily basis). However, typically, in coercive and controlling relationships, the abuse is persistent and sustained over a long period of time with little let-up.

Next, consider if your partner engages in these same problematic behaviors in other areas of their life or in their non-romantic relationships—with friends, family, and coworkers. Again, you are looking for a trend. For example, if your partner is overly critical of you, there is a good chance they tend to be hypercritical of others. Maybe it's not to the same extent or severity, but these behaviors are probably observable in other settings. Consider how they speak to others—their tone and word choice. Think about how they navigate conflict or disagreements in their other relationships or their ability to effectively manage their emotions.

While we are all human and all capable of making mistakes and having moments in our lives that we are not necessarily proud of, the emotionally abusive partner has a difficult time correcting their errors and changing their behavior. Because of their emotional immaturity and their lack of insight and empathy, they will continue to engage in the same behaviors again, and again, and again. Their behaviors have a pattern and are persistent in nature. And when there is a pattern, there is a problem. I know this process is difficult and can bring up so many unpleasant feelings. So, as you continue, try to be gentle with yourself and take as much time as you need to feel and hold space for these feelings.

Exercise: Pause and Reflect

Reflect on your partner's behavior throughout your relationship. Take some time to identify each of the different problematic or concerning behaviors you have observed or have been subjected to and consider their frequency and if there has been a pattern.

Journal exercise, Option 1: If you are in a relationship, create a log and write down every new occurrence of a behavior you are concerned about. Regularly review your log and consider if there is a pattern.

Example: *If you are concerned about your partner's possessiveness, write down every instance you observe this behavior (i.e., "Monday: he reprimanded me for talking to my male neighbor. Tuesday: he commented on me being friends with my male coworker on social media.").*

Journal exercise, Option 2: If you are no longer in your relationship, make a list of all the different instances of abusive behavior that occurred throughout the relationship. Play the relationship back in your mind as if it were a movie and take notes on their behavior from start to finish. Notice if there were certain behaviors you might have disregarded earlier on and now recognize as being part of a pattern.

Example: "1. On our fourth date, my ex made lots of comments about other men looking at me. 2. About two months into our relationship, my ex questioned my relationship with a male colleague and asked multiple times if we had ever dated despite me telling him we hadn't."

Don't Be Fooled by Superficial and Short-Term Changes

Many times, when an emotionally abusive partner is confronted about their problematic behavior and presented with an ultimatum (i.e., a potential breakup or divorce), they vow they will change and that things will be different moving forward. In some cases, EAPs stay true to their word. They will take the feedback seriously and do the actual work (such as going to therapy or seeking outside support) and they make lasting changes. However, this outcome is quite rare and typically the exception. In most cases, changes made by the EAP are short-term.

It can often feel like you're in a relationship with a toddler. You walk in on them coloring on the wall, you tell them to stop, and they do. But the moment you leave the room, they go back to coloring. EAPs will often promise that they will take serious action and do things, like "go to therapy." These promises can feel really encouraging to you, especially if the EAP has been resistant to changing or taking accountability in the past. Unfortunately, these promises are typically empty, and the EAP is mostly talk. You might have heard your EAP say they "want to go to therapy," but they don't have the time or haven't found a therapist yet. There is always some excuse or some reason why therapy isn't working out. And when the EAP does "go to therapy," their participation is minimal and short-lived. The EAP will often go to therapy for the sake of being able to *say* that they went to therapy or "tried it." But when it comes down to actual changes in their behavior, it's limited. They *might* curb some of their abusive tendencies, like criticizing you less or apologizing more and taking more ownership of their problematic behaviors, but the abuse persists.

You might feel misled or deceived by the EAP because these gestures feel performative and superficial. Here is the hard truth: changes in the EAP's behavior usually *are* superficial. This is because their motivation is extrinsic, not intrinsic. When someone is intrinsically motivated, their motivation is fueled by their internal drive (Morris et al. 2022). They change because they find personal benefit and gain in changing their behavior or doing things differently. They will seek therapy because they recognize the value of addressing and taking care of their mental health. They want to better themselves, be a better partner, and have a healthier relationship.

However, when someone is extrinsically motivated, their motivation is fueled by the desire for external rewards or to avoid punishment or consequence (Morris et al. 2022). This means that the EAP is usually motivated by positive feedback from their partner or the avoidance of a breakup. While extrinsic motivation is not necessarily bad and can lead to long-lasting change, if the EAP is motivated solely by external rewards, the changes in behavior are less likely to stick. Once they get what they want (i.e., praise or acknowledgment from their partner for the changes they have made), they are likely to slip back into their old patterns because they don't see their abusive behavior as being inherently wrong or problematic.

You Can't Change Them

If you've bent over backward trying to change your partner and/or improve the relationship, you are not alone. Many people fall victim to the belief that they can change the EAP and influence the course of the relationship. This comes from a false sense of control. Maybe you've set up therapy appointments for your partner, planned fun date nights, or taken on new financial responsibilities. Or maybe you have done everything that has been asked of you by your partner, from changing your appearance to ending friendships. Most likely, these efforts didn't yield the results you were hoping for, which has probably been so frustrating and disappointing because you worked so hard for things to be better.

The reality is that the EAP has their own free will and you cannot control their behavior. You cannot control your partner's perceptions and the core beliefs they maintain about themselves and the world at large. You cannot control how they think and feel. And you cannot control their level of motivation and insight. A healthy relationship requires both partners to be equally invested and involved and to assume responsibility for their own behaviors. It doesn't matter how committed you are or how much you love your partner. If your partner doesn't believe there is a real problem in the relationship or that their behavior is harmful, there is nothing *you* can do to improve the health of the relationship or change the outcome.

The Costs of Your Relationship

Other aspects to consider when confronting the reality of your relationship are the costs. Regardless of how you choose to define or label your relationship, you cannot deny the costs when you are being abused or mistreated—because there are always costs. Below, I've listed some of the costs that can come from being in a relationship with an EAP:

- The ability to speak and express yourself freely
- Your support system and important friendships and non-romantic relationships that existed prior to this relationship
- Your confidence and self-esteem
- Your sense of autonomy and independence
- Your sense of safety
- Your personal identity
- Financial independence
- Personal goals and ambitions
- Work and job opportunities
- Healthy body image

- The ability to engage in hobbies and interests that you used to enjoy
- Your mental health and happiness

Reading through this list, which of these costs resonates with you most? Are there any other things you have lost or have had to sacrifice because of your relationship? Being honest with yourself and taking inventory of these costs is important if you want to truly break free from this abusive partner. I know that confronting the reality of your relationship isn't an easy task. This is why having and practicing self-compassion is crucial in your healing. To do so, you need to offer yourself the same compassion you would to a child or close friend. In this next exercise, you will have the opportunity to practice self-compassion.

Exercise: What Would You Say to Your Younger Self?

For this exercise, find a picture of your younger self (ideally, a printed photograph). With this picture in front of you or image in mind, think about what you would say to this younger self if they were in the same relationship. What would you say to them if they were in or leaving a relationship with a partner who had been abusive? First and foremost, try saying these words out loud—speak to your younger self. Then, if you feel inclined, write these same words down and keep the picture in a space that is nearby and safe. Go back to this photo and repeat these same exact words to yourself whenever you are struggling and need more loving words.

If this exercise was difficult, that's okay. Many people struggle with having self-compassion. In chapter 8, we will talk more about the importance of self-compassion and how to further develop your self-compassion practice.

Let's Recap

Denying your reality and getting hung up on the fantasy version of your partner and relationship is common and a natural defense mechanism. This denial helps you cope with situations that are stressful and confusing. However, living in this fantasy version is ultimately harmful and disempowering. To fully break free from a relationship with an emotionally abusive partner, you need to acknowledge the reality. This reality reckoning includes: (1) recognizing the persistent and unchanging patterns of behavior of the EAP; (2) being aware of the EAP's lack of motivation; (3) accepting your lack of control and influence; and (4) taking inventory of the costs that come with staying in an abusive dynamic.

Chapter 5

Leaving Your Emotionally Abusive Partner

Many people assume that leaving an emotionally abusive partner is the *easy* part. That leaving an abusive dynamic is the obvious solution, a no-brainer, and can be done swiftly. But ending a relationship is never easy. Walking away from someone you have invested in and built a life with is almost always difficult. When you love or care about someone—their feelings and well-being—the last thing you want to do is hurt them. This even includes walking away from someone who has mistreated or abused you.

Yes, breaking up with an abuser is the best thing for you. Yes, breaking up with an abuser is empowering. Yes, breaking up with an abuser will offer you some peace and relief. But ending a relationship with an EAP is also much more nuanced—much like the abuse you endured in the relationship itself. You will probably have many conflicting thoughts and feelings. One minute, you might feel sad, and then the next, angry. One minute, you might be cursing your ex to a friend, and the next, wondering if you should reach out to them to see how they are doing. And that's okay. You are allowed to oscillate and feel different things, but it is important to hold steady on your decision.

Additionally, because the EAP is emotionally immature, they probably won't make the breakup any easier for you. They may challenge your decision and use the same coercive tactics to manipulate you into staying. They may try to contact you or maintain some form of communication with you post breakup. There is also the possibility they could become vindictive and engage in post-breakup abuse.

In this chapter, you'll learn about some of the hurdles you might encounter after ending the relationship, including potential pushback from the EAP, unsolicited feedback or opinions from friends and family, and self-doubt. You will then work to develop the skills you need to navigate the breakup and overcome these hurdles. You'll also continue your self-compassion practice—this decision and breakup process can be taxing and weigh on you.

Expect Pushback

• Aiden's Story

Aiden decided he wanted to divorce his wife. There wasn't a day that she didn't criticize him or put him down. She mocked his hobbies, interests, and sense of humor. She also made it a point to isolate him from his family and regularly talked poorly about them—despite them always being very kind and welcoming. She refused to let him visit with them or have them be a part of their life. The abuse only escalated when they had their kids. After years of conflict, he was finally at his breaking point and had come to terms with the reality: things were not going to change or get any better.

Divorce had come up quite a few times in passing—usually because his partner would threaten divorce during fights or arguments—so, he was hopeful his partner would be on board. To him, it was very clear that things weren't working and he believed she would feel similarly—after all, she never seemed happy or satisfied with him or their marriage. Unfortunately, he was wrong. When Aiden informed his wife of his decision to end their marriage, she pushed back. She called him selfish and guilted him for even having the thought of divorce. She told him that divorce was not on the table and that they needed to do "whatever it takes" to stay together. Her reaction was confusing to him and made him start to doubt his judgment and decision.

The emotionally abusive partner doesn't change after the breakup. They are the same person and have the same personality. This means that they will most likely engage in the same, or at least very similar, problematic behaviors during and after the breakup. They will have a strong emotional reaction and most likely try to say and do things to manipulate you into staying. The following are some of the protesting behaviors that can occur when you initiate a breakup with an EAP. Later in the chapter, you will learn how to take control of the situation.

Tantruming: Tantruming occurs when the EAP has an emotional outburst in response to the breakup. This can involve wailing, cursing, yelling, threatening, or engaging in self-injurious behavior, like hitting themselves. They may also make self-deprecating statements and berate themselves—or even threaten suicide. They do this to seek comfort and validation. They want to shift the attention from you and your needs to theirs.

Example: *"I don't deserve happiness!" "I'm a bad person who can't do anything right!"*

Objecting: Objecting is when the EAP objects to your decision or boundary and tries to will you into changing your mind. They will often try to challenge your feelings and reasoning and make you doubt your own judgment. If the EAP objects to a breakup, they may insist that breaking up is a two-person decision and that there needs to be a mutual understanding and agreement.

Example: *"We can't break up!" "Are you sure about this? I don't think you've thought it through."*

Blaming: The EAP will often try to blame you for the demise of the relationship. Because they struggle with taking accountability, it's easier for them to point their finger at you. They will argue that you are at fault and responsible for the toxicity of the relationship. The EAP will do this when they want to come out of the breakup as the victor.

Examples: *"You're the reason why things got so bad." "You're just going to give up?!"*

Coaxing: Coaxing, also known as hoovering, occurs when the EAP tries to win you back or suck you back in. Think of this as their last-ditch effort, their "hail Mary." They might do this through compliments, words of affirmation, grand gestures, and promises that they will change and that things will be different. Coaxing typically occurs when the EAP has been able to sway you or dodge a breakup before. They don't take the breakup seriously and believe they can and will get you to change your mind.

Examples: *"I promise, things will be different." "Let's go on a vacation. Maybe we just need some time to relax one-on-one." "You are the love of my life—we have to work this out!"*

Testing: Even when you have "successfully" ended the relationship, the EAP will often try to test you and push the boundary. For example, if you expressed a need for going no-contact, they are likely to try and test this limit. This can involve them fishing for communication—reaching out to you to "check in," address a logistical item (like picking up their mail), or seek support when they are in distress.

Examples: *"I know we aren't together, but you're the only person I can really talk to." "I think I may have left some of my things at your place. Can I come over?"*

Regardless of their intention, these protest behaviors are inherently manipulative. Like their coercion tactics, protesting is another way to evoke empathy and emotions and distract you from your needs and decision to end the relationship. What's important to remember is that you have the right to end the relationship, even if it doesn't make sense to the EAP. You don't have to wait for the EAP to be on board or at peace with a decision that is imperative to your mental health and well-being. It's your decision to make—don't let these protest behaviors keep you hostage.

Do you notice any of these behaviors in your relationship? Spend some time journaling or taking a moment to reflect on how this makes you feel and what you can control when these things happen. Next, we will discuss different approaches you might consider to counter these behaviors and stand your ground.

Take Control

- ### Mercedes's Story

    Mercedes was ready to end the relationship with her partner. She had been in denial for some time, hoping that something would change in her relationship. But through the work she had done in therapy and multiple candid conversations with her closest friends, she had come to accept the reality: her partner was abusive and was never going to change. The question now for Mercedes was: when and how would they break up?

    "Maybe I'll just wait for him to end it," she thought. Mercedes and her partner had talked about breaking up before. Her partner would regularly make comments about how life would be a lot simpler with someone else, someone "easier." He would criticize her often and tell her how easy it would be for him to meet someone else. To Mercedes, him ending the relationship would be most ideal. Then she wouldn't have to worry about him having a negative reaction or becoming vindictive. But deep down, a part of her knew he probably would never actually follow through.

In an ideal world, the EAP would have the insight to recognize that the relationship is just not working out. The breakup would be mutual and both parties would feel good and at peace with the decision, and you could exit peacefully. Unfortunately, this isn't the reality. While the EAP might threaten a breakup or communicate their own unhappiness, this is actually a control tactic meant to keep you feeling insecure and wanting to please them. They don't really want to break up because the relationship has been working for *them*. This means that *you* are going to have to take control. When you have become accustomed to taking the back seat in your relationship and your partner has been making all the calls and setting all the terms, taking control can feel uncomfortable and unnatural; however, it's the only way you can truly break free.

Witnessing the EAP during the breakup can be hard. It's common for individuals leaving an abusive dynamic to experience guilt or feel a sense of responsibility for their partner's emotional distress. In fact, many individuals avoid breaking up because of the potential pushback and/or concern for their partner's emotional well-being. But the reality is that the EAP is going to feel how they are going to feel. You cannot prevent them from being mad or upset or influence their perception of you or the relationship post breakup. So, instead, it's best to focus on what you *can* control, which includes how you communicate with the EAP, how you choose to respond (or not respond) to their reactivity, and what you do moving forward to protect yourself and prioritize your needs and healing.

Assertive Communication

Being assertive can be difficult with an EAP. Most likely (at least, up until now), they probably have dominated most conversations or made it difficult for you to effectively set limits and express your feelings and needs. However, when you break up with the EAP, it's important to be assertive and take a firm stance. When you are speaking to the EAP, be honest and direct about your decision to end the relationship. Do not be vague or try to sugarcoat things, as this will leave things open for interpretation. This doesn't mean you have to be unkind. Being assertive just means being clear about what you want and how you feel and not giving them any room for rebuttal. Below are examples of nonassertive breakup statements (what not to do) and assertive breakup statements.

Nonassertive Statements

"I've been thinking...I don't think this is going to work out between us."

"I don't think either of us is happy. We would probably be better apart."

"What if we took a break for a little bit?"

"I think we should break up."

"I don't think I'm the partner you want."

These nonassertive statements are not effective because they are indirect and communicate indecisiveness, like the decision has not yet been made and there is room for negotiation. When you talk about the breakup as more of an idea or suggestion or ask your partner for their thoughts or input, this opens things up for discussion.

Assertive Statements

"I have made the decision to break up."

"I can no longer see you."

"This relationship is harmful to me, and I need to leave."

"I am breaking up with you."

"I am ending this relationship."

These assertive statements are clear and concise. They communicate that a decision has already been made and it is not up for further discussion.

While most breakup conversations will, of course, be lengthier, what's most important is that you communicate exactly what you intend to happen moving forward. This decision does not need to be mutual: while feelings may be hurt, you have to do what's in *your* best interest.

You may also need to repeat the same assertive statement more than once—especially if you have tried to break up with them before.

Exercise: Pause and Reflect

Take a moment to journal about or reflect on these assertive communication tools. How might you start to implement them? What would that look like for you?

• Stacy's Story

Stacy had finally ended her relationship with her emotionally abusive partner of over three years. It took her some time, but through the support of her friends and family, she gained the courage to take control and end the relationship that had been hurting her for so long. Her partner didn't take it well and said some pretty horrible things during their last conversation. But, at the end of the day, she was just relieved that it was finally over. Unfortunately, her ex wasn't ready to completely cut ties.

Stacy and her ex had adopted a dog together earlier in their relationship. Stacy had basically been the primary caregiver. The dog had lived with her, and she paid for most of the dog's expenses—food, vet bills, etc. So, Stacy had concluded it was only natural for her to keep the dog; her ex ultimately agreed. However, shortly after they broke up, it became apparent that Stacy's ex would use the dog as an excuse to maintain contact. Stacy's ex regularly asked to visit the dog. Out of guilt, Stacy usually conceded. But this made their breakup a little sticky. Stacy and her ex would end up spending time together during these dog visitations. Most of the time, the conversations were fun and light, but at other times during these visits, there was obvious tension. Stacy really wanted to be able to move on and heal—but this current dynamic made it difficult. She wasn't sure how much longer she could do this with her ex.

Setting and Reinforcing Boundaries

Some EAPs will be receptive to the breakup. They might not like it and may be upset, but they will accept the decision. Others will protest and/or try to weasel their way back into your life after the breakup. Therefore, it's important to set boundaries—firm limits that communicate exactly what you expect from your ex moving forward in terms of your level of contact. Here are some examples of boundaries you might set with an EAP:

- Going 100 percent "no-contact" with your ex (no calls, texts, emails, or communication through social media)

- Communicating only through email about logistical items (i.e., bills, moving)

- Unfriending/unfollowing them on social media

- Ending contact with your ex's family and friends

- Canceling shared plans/trips

- Engaging only in conversations that are necessary for co-parenting or custody-related items

- Agreeing to communicate solely through a co-parent communication app

Even if the EAP does not understand the boundary, has hurt feelings, or pushes back, it's important that you stand your ground. If you are wishy-washy or do not enforce the boundary, this communicates flexibility and that your boundaries can be challenged.

Below are tips to help you set boundaries with the EAP after the breakup:

1. **Be assertive:** Be clear and direct with the EAP about what *your* limit is. Do you want to completely cut ties or end all communication? Do you need to communicate strictly through email? Don't beat around the bush—clearly state your limits and the exact behavior you expect.

2. **Expect pushback:** Try to have realistic expectations and anticipate pushback. Asserting a boundary doesn't guarantee that it will be honored or respected. Again, based on what you already know about the EAP and what you observed during the relationship, they are most likely going to have some emotional reaction or try to challenge any boundaries you set. They could use guilt or completely ignore the boundary. Remember, this isn't personal and that doesn't mean that your boundary is wrong or invalid. Regardless of the response, maintain the boundary.

3. **Avoid overexplaining:** As someone who has empathy and compassion, you may feel inclined to explain, justify your boundary, or even apologize to the EAP for setting this limit. However, you are setting a boundary as a means of self-preservation and don't owe the EAP any explanation. Additionally, when you try to explain yourself and your position, it can appear as if you are having a discussion with the EAP and that the boundary is up for debate. Do not give the EAP any more opportunities to assert control or influence or make you question your decision. Your boundary is your boundary and that is all the EAP needs to know.

4. **Prepare to reinforce the boundary:** When you set a boundary, prepare to follow through and reinforce it. This means that if the EAP does not respect your boundary and crosses a line, there needs to be a consequence. This consequence is up to you—but it should demonstrate that you are serious about your boundary and will not tolerate it being crossed. Examples of potential consequences include blocking the EAP's phone number or deciding to end all contact if you were open to contact before. (We will be talking more about blocking the EAP in a bit.)

5. **Remind yourself of your "why":** If you start to doubt yourself and the boundary you have set, remind yourself of your "why." Ask yourself, "Why did I set the boundary in the first place?" or "What was the purpose of the boundary?" I imagine that

you are setting a boundary to protect yourself and take your power back. Additionally, if/when the EAP pushes back, this feedback can serve as a reminder of why the boundary was needed to begin with. By reminding yourself of your why, you'll feel more confident in your decision and judgment and be able to communicate the boundary with greater self-assurance.

It's important to note that if you are in a situation in which you are required to co-parent with the EAP, boundaries will probably look a little different. Going no-contact, for example, is not feasible when you need to coordinate schedules or discuss the needs of your child/children. Therefore, your boundaries might be fluid or exist with exceptions (i.e., if there is an emergency and you need to call the EAP).

• Talia's Story

Talia had been broken up with her partner for just over a month. For a while, he'd been mostly respectful of the "no contact" boundary she had set. She had received a couple text messages here and there from her ex, including a "happy birthday" text, but they had seemed harmless, and she wasn't too worried that the behavior would escalate. However, one night, her ex called to rehash an argument that they had while they were still together. Again, he was accusing her of cheating on him (she hadn't). This call, of course, went nowhere. Talia left the call feeling anxious and also angry at herself for even answering the phone to begin with.

The following day, Talia shared what happened with a close friend and the friend suggested blocking his phone number. Talia knew that her friend was probably right and that blocking his number would provide her with some sense of peace, but she was also ambivalent. How could she block this person whom she had been involved with for so long and cared for? Ultimately, Talia blocked his phone number and him on social media as well. She did feel some guilt, but was mostly relieved that she wouldn't have to engage in that same argument ever again and that she could finally move on.

Creating More Distance

Back in the day when social media was nonexistent and we didn't have smartphones, we were able to make a relatively clean break after a breakup. While there was some possibility of running into or crossing paths with an ex, they were generally inaccessible—we had the time and space to move on and heal. Unfortunately, breaking up is not as straightforward these days. One of the biggest barriers for individuals trying to break free and recover from their emotionally abusive relationship is the virtual tie they maintain with the EAP post breakup.

When you are still virtually connected to an ex, especially an EAP, it can be difficult to fully move on because, in a lot of ways, you are leaving the door open for some form of relationship and/or communication. This can make things messy and drag out the process. Additionally, if the EAP is unrelenting and engaging in post-breakup abuse (trying to control, coerce, and hurt you even after the relationship has ended) or if staying virtually connected to the EAP is going to cause you even the slightest bit of distress, it's important to weigh these costs. Your sense of safety and general well-being need to be your top priority.

So, what would creating distance look like? This all depends on the situation and what *you* need. Here are some options:

- Delete your ex's phone number from your phone
- Block your ex's phone number, email address, social media accounts, etc.
- Unfriend or unfollow your ex on social media
- Change your phone number
- Limit your communication to a co-parent communication app

While some of these options might feel extreme, you have every right to do whatever you need to do to protect yourself and have peace of mind.

The Presence of Self-Doubt

- ## Jenna's Story

    For the longest time, Jenna was able to ignore her partner's abusive tendencies, chalking it up to his neurotic personality and perfectionism. But she had reached her breaking point when her partner started to monitor and criticize her food choices and weight. Because they lived together, she went to stay with family while she looked for a new place. During her stay, she finally opened up to a close family member about her relationship and the abuse she experienced. It felt good having someone listen to her and validate her experiences.

    However, when she was alone and had too much time to herself, she started to question her decision. Now, she would have to live alone and start dating again. Did she really have it in her to start over? Maybe her partner wasn't that abusive. Maybe he really did just want her to be healthy. Maybe she could learn how to ignore some of his comments or let it roll off her back. After all, they had built a life together.

Self-doubt is normal and to be expected when ending a relationship with an EAP. You are going to feel conflicted and there are going to be moments when you question yourself. When you have been immersed in a coercive, controlling, and emotionally abusive relationship and have been systematically belittled, ridiculed, and criticized, you lose confidence in your ability to think critically, problem solve, and make important decisions. When you are used to your partner being the authority of everything, it can be hard to trust yourself.

Additionally, when you are experiencing ambivalence or have conflicting feelings about your partner and relationship, this can further ramp up any self-doubt you might have. Missing the EAP or grieving the relationship is confusing. You might ask yourself, "If this was the best decision for me, why do I feel so bad?" This, however, doesn't mean that your decision is wrong or that you made a mistake. Like any big life decision, it's normal to experience some feelings of doubt. But this doubt is only a fear response and doesn't have to take the driver's seat.

Overcoming Self-Doubt

Once you are able to identify these moments of self-doubt and recognize it as a fear response, you'll find that it becomes easier to overcome. Next, you'll learn about some of the things you can do to conquer this self-doubt and reestablish trust in yourself.

Call It Out

One strategy to overcome self-doubt is to call it out for what it is: a fear-based response. By acknowledging that your thoughts of self-doubt are simply fear-based, you can see them a bit more clearly and with more objectivity. Instead of reacting impulsively or making decisions from a place of fear (i.e., responding to a hostile text message from the EAP, breaking your own "no contact" boundary), you will be able to work through this self-doubt and feel more grounded in your decision to leave (Harris 2008).

As an example, let's say that one of your intrusive thoughts that feeds this feeling of self-doubt is *Maybe the relationship wasn't as bad as I thought it was*. There are different ways you could respond to and call out your self-doubt.

- **Make it a story.** Tell yourself, "I am telling myself the 'my relationship wasn't as bad as I thought it was' story again and I know it's just a story."

- **Name it.** Say, "I am having a fear-based thought that *My relationship wasn't as bad as I thought it was*."

- **Notice it.** Inform yourself, "I notice I am having a thought of self-doubt."

Try these strategies out and decide which one works best for you. Ultimately, the goal is for you to create some distance between yourself and these thoughts and not become too consumed with any self-doubt that may arise.

Practice Self-Compassion

Another strategy to help you cope with and overcome self-doubt is to be loving and compassionate toward yourself. As discussed in chapter 4, self-compassion is crucial for healing. Having compassion tends to be easy for us when it comes to other people. We are way more patient, nurturing, and encouraging with others, especially with the people we love and care for most. If your close friend were to reach out to you, upset that they were yelled at by their abusive partner, chances are you wouldn't tell them, "You probably deserved it" or "What did you do to make them so angry?" No, you would probably hold space for them, allow them to vent and express how they were feeling, and then provide comforting or supporting words. You would see that they were hurting and, without any hesitation, respond with compassion.

Having compassion for ourselves, however, is a whole different story. When we make a mistake or do something embarrassing, we turn to shame—kicking ourselves while we are already down. We are more inclined to shame ourselves rather than treat ourselves with kindness and understanding. But shame is not helpful or productive. While we think it may motivate us to change our behavior or do "better," shame only fuels more shame. And when you indulge your thoughts of self-doubt, you only give them more power. So, instead, try to offer yourself gentle and supportive words that are encouraging and evoke more confidence in yourself.

Like any skill, self-compassion can be learned. Here are some examples of how you can use self-compassion in your everyday life:

- Speak to yourself like you would a young child (be very gentle, patient, and kind).

- When you notice yourself becoming self-critical, remind yourself that you are human and make mistakes.

- Honor and validate your feelings (i.e., tell yourself, "It's okay to feel sad/angry/disappointed/embarrassed").

- Use gentle touch by giving yourself a warm embrace, caressing your arms, or holding your hands to your heart.

- Write a letter to yourself as though you were writing to your best friend who is going through a similar difficult situation.

Self-compassion is the antidote to shame. When you can see yourself as human—flawed and imperfect—and honor and hold space for your feelings, you become more resilient in every aspect of your life. You feel a lot more grounded and rational because you are not as inclined to internalize these adverse experiences or berate yourself. Below is an activity to further support your self-compassion practice as you navigate or exit the emotionally abusive relationship.

Exercise: Loving Letter

In your journal or on a piece of paper, write a loving letter to yourself that is supportive of your decision to end your relationship. Write this letter with the intention to validate your feelings, provide comforting words, and instill confidence. Additionally, if you find this exercise challenging or have a difficult time being compassionate toward yourself, similar to the exercise in chapter 3, consider how you would speak to your younger self and the language and words you would use with them. Or write this loving letter as if you were writing it to a close friend or loved one who was in the exact same situation. For even more guidance and structure, use the following template below, which is available at http://www.newharbinger.com/55480.

Loving Letter Template

Dear (your name here),

I'm so sorry for what you went through and that you were in a relationship that was harmful to you. I know you are feeling so many things including (list all feelings here).

I hope you know that every single one of your feelings is valid and allowed to be felt.

I also want you to know how extremely proud I am of you for making the difficult decision to leave. That took a lot of courage. And while there may be times that you question or second-guess your decision, try to remind yourself of your "why." You left the relationship because (list every reason here and include examples): (i.e., "He made you feel like you couldn't do anything right," "You never felt like you could be yourself," "She didn't let you spend time with [insert favorite person"]).

Remember, just like everyone else, you deserve a healthy relationship—a relationship that makes you feel safe, secure, and accepted.

Love,

(your name here)

Once you have written your loving letter, make sure you have easy access to it. For example, if you wrote it in your journal, you could take a picture of it and keep it in your phone. Go back to this letter and read it to yourself anytime you begin to question your decision or experience moments of self-doubt. You can also refer back to this loving letter if and when the EAP tries to reel you back into the relationship. Think of this letter as a tool to help you feel more grounded and centered, reminding you of your worth and ability to make decisions that reflect who you are and what you deserve in a relationship.

Let's Recap

Ending a relationship is never easy. It's hard to part ways with someone you love or care about or a relationship that you worked so hard to preserve. When you end a relationship with an EAP, there is an added layer of stress because of their emotional immaturity and the pushback you are likely to experience from them. Additionally, you might find yourself struggling with self-doubt and questioning your decision to remove yourself from the relationship, which can make it difficult for you to assert and maintain firm boundaries post breakup. These obstacles are part of the aftereffects of being in a relationship with an EAP, which we will explore in the next chapter.

Chapter 6

Recognizing the Aftereffects of Emotional Abuse

While it would be ideal if the breakup itself with the emotionally abusive partner concluded this chapter of your life, that's not quite the case. This experience is actually a two-parter. First, there is the breakup itself—which, as discussed in chapter 5, isn't always as straightforward as you might hope it would be. Then comes the trauma recovery and healing process post abuse. Yes, that's right: what you experienced and endured in a relationship with an EAP *was* traumatic. Unfortunately, while you are not responsible for the abuse, you are responsible for your healing and doing the work you need to do to move forward and live the life that you deserve—that all of us deserve. The good news is that you are resilient and have the capacity to do this very work and overcome the trauma and aftereffects of the abuse.

In this next chapter, you will learn the definition of *trauma* and how unhealed trauma can have an impact on your body and mind. You'll understand the different types of trauma responses that you may be experiencing. Then, you'll learn about the role of grief, unraveling how to reconcile this grief and the relief that you are also likely to experience, which can be confusing. You'll also have more opportunities to self-reflect, self-soothe, and continue your self-compassion practice.

Understanding Trauma

- ### Allie's Story

    Allie had sought out therapy because she was struggling with dating. She'd been broken up with her long-term partner for over a year and was ready to be in a relationship again. She had been dating a new guy for just over three months and things had been going well—at least, during the first few weeks. More recently, she noticed that she was experiencing a lot of anxiety around this new relationship. She was distrusting of this new person and experienced panic when she didn't hear back from him. Despite him providing her with regular reassurance and validation and being consistent, she couldn't trust him and didn't know why.

    After a few therapy sessions, it became clear that Allie's anxiety was a by-product of her last relationship. Allie's ex had been emotionally abusive and had been hot and cold with her throughout their relationship. One minute, he would be basically worshipping her and telling her how much he loved and cared for her, and the next, he would be giving her the silent treatment and criticizing her for how she dressed and how she spent her free time. Allie had thought she had moved on from her ex—after all, they hadn't spoken since they broke up. But, through therapy and self-reflection, it was apparent that she was carrying the trauma from her past relationship into her present. She was navigating this new relationship from a place of fear and trying to protect herself from being hurt again by this new partner.

If you are hesitant to describe your experience as "traumatic" or use the word "trauma" in reference to your relationship with an emotionally abusive partner, you are not alone. Many individuals who have experienced emotional abuse struggle with this term. A lot of people hesitate to use the word "trauma" because their relationship didn't involve physical abuse or wasn't "as bad" as other people's experiences. While it's not required for you to label or categorize your relationship as "traumatic," acknowledging the traumatic nature of your emotionally abusive relationship can be validating and help you make sense of the impact it may have on you as well as how you navigate new relationships post abuse. So, let's start with the basics by defining and understanding the nature of trauma.

Trauma can be understood as any stressful or disturbing event, experience, or set of circumstances that threatens your sense of mental and physical safety and general well-being. Here are some things to know about trauma:

- Trauma is subjective. What may be traumatic to one person might not be traumatic to another. For example, two people can be in the exact same car accident and perceive or experience the event very differently.

- Unhealed or unprocessed trauma can result in an overactive sympathetic nervous system and chemical changes in our brain that influence our cognition (how we think), behavior (how we interact with the world and respond to stressors), and attachment (how we relate to others and experience our relationships).

- Trauma is stored in the mind and body at a subconscious level. Therefore, "the past is present" even when you are not consciously thinking about a particular trauma or disturbing event (Shapiro 2012, 10).

- You can experience trauma and be impacted by it without having a diagnosis of posttraumatic stress disorder (PTSD). You don't need to have a diagnosis of PTSD to validate your experience.

Emotionally Abusive Relationships and Complex Trauma

Trauma can be distinguished into distinct categories. *Acute trauma* describes single event experiences, such as a car accident, natural disaster, or sudden loss of a loved one. *Chronic trauma* describes when someone experiences repeated or recurring traumatic events, such as living in poverty, childhood abuse, or being in combat over an extended period of time. And then there is *complex trauma*. You may be thinking, *What type of trauma isn't complex?* Trauma is considered complex when an individual experiences "encompassing prolonged and repeated harmful events that typically occur in the interpersonal sphere" (van Nieuwenhove and Meganck 2017). What makes complex trauma distinct is its interpersonal nature. To simplify this definition, complex trauma is the result of the following:

- Multiple traumatic events or experiences that compound over time

- Distress or abuse that occurs in a relationship dynamic between two people

- Trauma that occurs between an individual and an attachment figure (i.e., parent, mentor, close friend, partner, etc.)

Emotional abuse is a form of complex trauma because there is almost always more than one occurrence and it typically persists over an extended period of time. When the person in your life who is supposed to be safe and loving becomes the person who hurts you, this experience can be completely destabilizing and results in heightened anxiety and fear, low self-esteem and self-worth, challenges with trust and intimacy, avoidant behaviors, and feelings of hopelessness and helplessness.

Trauma Responses Post Abuse

Ultimately, the trauma of your emotionally abusive relationship has aftereffects that can persist if they go unaddressed. Next, you'll learn about these trauma responses in greater detail. As you read through the different trauma responses, take note of the ones that you may be experiencing.

Heightened Anxiety

When you have been in a long-term relationship that lacked stability and safety, it's common to experience heightened anxiety even after the relationship has ended. This heightened anxiety is the outcome of the persistent fear and chronic stress experienced during the relationship. You operate from a place of hypervigilance, seeking potential danger even when there is no threat present. Here are some examples of how your anxiety might manifest:

- Feeling restless and unsafe in situations and environments that are safe

- Impulsivity and self-sabotaging behaviors in new relationships (i.e., ending a relationship out of fear, wrongfully accusing a new partner/date of doing something hurtful)

- Regular worrying and obsessing about your relationships to the point that it causes distress

- Reexperiencing the same or similar feelings of anxiety you experienced in your relationship with the EAP in a new, safe relationship (i.e., a new partner respectfully disagrees with you, and you experience a wave of panic)

Low Self-Esteem and Self-Worth

When you have been immersed in an abusive relationship, how you view and see yourself often becomes skewed. It can almost feel as though you have been brainwashed because your thoughts and self-concept reflect the abuse and beliefs of the EAP. For example, if you were regularly criticized for your weight or physical appearance, your body image would likely be negatively impacted. This feedback can be incredibly damaging and result in low self-esteem and sense of self-worth. Here are some examples of how low self-esteem and self-worth can manifest:

- Engaging in negative self-talk (berating yourself or putting yourself down)

- General feelings of inadequacy and feeling "not good enough"
- Seeking external validation from others (including romantic partners)
- People-pleasing behaviors (i.e., going above and beyond to be liked and avoid upsetting others)
- Taking the blame or responsibility for things that are not your fault

Challenges with Trust and Intimacy

Being in an emotionally abusive relationship can cause general feelings of mistrust due to the betrayal experienced in the relationship. The person who was supposed to love, care for, and protect you became the very person who mistreated you and violated your trust. This lack of trust can cause you to question the intentions or sincerity of others. It can also cause you to question yourself—your judgment and your ability to navigate relationships. Here are some examples of how mistrust might manifest in your everyday life:

- Overanalyzing interpersonal interactions
- Questioning a new or prospective partner's motives or level of commitment
- Being more reserved and closed off in new relationships
- Not feeling confident in your decision-making abilities
- Questioning your intuition or gut feeling

Avoidant Behaviors

When you have experienced trauma, it's common to avoid people, places, situations, and experiences that resemble or remind you of the traumatic event(s). Therefore, after emotional abuse, you'll probably notice yourself being avoidant—trying to dodge anything and everything that could cause you similar feelings of hurt and pain. Here are some ways you may be experiencing avoidance:

- Swearing off dating or relationships completely

- Putting off difficult or sensitive conversations in your relationships out of fear of conflict

- Feeling numb or dissociative while dating and pursuing new relationships

- Increase in substance use/abuse to numb the feelings associated with the abuse

- Jumping into a new relationship before processing and healing from the abusive relationship

Hopelessness and Helplessness

Emotionally abusive relationships can make you feel completely out of control. When you worked so hard to improve the state of your relationship and be "better" for your partner, only to learn that nothing will ever be good enough for the EAP, you leave the relationship feeling discouraged and disempowered. You start losing faith in yourself and your ability to live a happy and meaningful life. Unfortunately, this mindset can lead you to feel hopeless and helpless. Here are some examples of how these feelings of hopelessness and helplessness might manifest:

- Having low expectations for others (including prospective partners)

- Maintaining a negative or pessimistic mentality about relationships (i.e., telling yourself, "I'm better off single" or "Relationships are a waste of time")

- Being unable to experience positive feelings or enjoy new relationships

Exercise: Pause and Reflect

Take a moment to consider your own behavior and day-to-day experiences post abuse. Is it possible that you are exhibiting trauma responses? Are you acting or navigating life as if you are still in the abusive relationship? If you are unsure, consider if there have been any significant changes in the following:

- Your general mood
- Your level of anxiety
- Your interpersonal relationships and interactions
- Your self-image
- Your general functioning

Grief After Emotional Abuse

• Daniela's Story

Daniela had been out of her emotionally abusive relationship for a few months now. Initially, she felt mostly relief—like a huge weight had been lifted off her. She was relieved that she didn't have to worry about her partner's mood all the time or if she was going to be criticized for something small, like how she loaded the dishwasher. She was also relieved that she could freely spend time with friends and wear whatever she wanted without being scrutinized by her ex. Then, after having some time to herself to self-reflect and come to terms with the extent of the abuse, she was angry. She was angry at her ex for how he mistreated her and how insecure he made her. And she was angry at herself for staying in the relationship for as long as she did.

    And then, after anger, came unexpected grief. Daniela grieved the good times she had with her ex—some of the trips they took together, times that they were able to laugh and enjoy each other's company without any conflict, and the holiday traditions they had made. Daniela also grieved her partner's friends and family, who had, over time, become her own.

This grief felt particularly uncomfortable and caused her a great deal of shame. She had a hard time understanding how she could grieve or miss the person who had been so awful to her. She was also worried about being judged by her family and friends and became less and less inclined to share her feelings. Daniela didn't know what to do with this grief.

In addition to the complex trauma you may experience from the emotionally abusive relationship, you are also likely to grieve. In this next section, you will learn about the different types of grief you might encounter post abuse. As you read, try to maintain an attitude of curiosity and nonjudgment.

Grieving the Loss of Relationships and Connections

You might grieve the relationships that were lost while you were in the relationship with the EAP. As discussed in chapter 3, when you are in a relationship that is all-consuming, it's hard to maintain your friendships and other non-romantic relationships. And even if you were able to maintain some of these connections, it's common for dynamics to shift and relationships to change. For example, you may not feel as close to some of your friends or as comfortable opening up to them as you had been in the past. Maybe you got cut off from your friends because they saw you go back and forth with your ex. Or perhaps you lost touch with a community you were previously part of because you were isolated.

After the relationship with the EAP ends, you might notice yourself thinking more about these relationships and becoming more aware of the absence of some of these connections that were important to you—and that's okay. Try to honor this grief and be gentle with yourself, as well as use this experience as an opportunity to learn and grow. You were in a relationship that isolated you and you did the best you could. While you can't go back in time, you can do things differently moving forward. You can reinvest in these connections and try to repair some of these relationships. It may take some time, but it can and will get better.

Grieving the Loss of Who You Were Before

As you now know, when you are in an emotionally abusive relationship, you go into survival mode—doing whatever it takes to avoid conflict with the EAP and keep the peace. Oftentimes, this involves you denying or changing parts of yourself to please or appease your partner—molding yourself into someone completely different. There's also a good chance that you abandoned some of the things that were important to you, the things that brought you joy or comfort. So, you might find yourself grieving the person you were before you met the EAP—before you were mistreated and abused.

Maybe this past version of you had been more hopeful and optimistic. Maybe you were more confident and secure in who you were. Maybe you felt more comfortable in your skin and carefree. Grieving these parts of you is normal. The good news is you can always return back to yourself and rediscover those parts of you that were abandoned. We will talk more about this in the coming chapters.

Grieving the Loss of Your Partner

You could also grieve your partner. Seems counterintuitive, right? Missing the very person who harmed you? But this is also common. Grieving the EAP and loss of the relationship can be uncomfortable and cause feelings of shame—especially when the people closest to you are unable to empathize or understand why you would grieve your abuser. But grief is a normal response to any kind of deep or meaningful loss, regardless of the circumstances.

Although the EAP is probably not the same person you first met or the person you came to develop strong feelings for or loved, you can still grieve them—or at least their "good" qualities and parts of the relationship that you valued. For example, you could grieve the companionship or the deep connection you once shared. You could also grieve the times when they were kind and sweet to you. Or you might grieve the loss of the friends and family you gained through your partner—the relationships you had to let go of once you ended your relationship with the EAP.

However, while this grief is normal, it's also important to keep in mind that just because you are grieving, it doesn't mean you made the wrong decision. To avoid getting lulled back into the relationship or abusive cycle, pair the "good" times with the "bad" to keep a more balanced memory of this person who hurt you.

Processing Your Grief

Grief is expansive. There will probably be other things you will grieve as you move on from this relationship. Other losses you might grieve post abuse include the following:

- Time that was lost
- Your youthfulness
- Unfulfilled hopes and plans that you had for the relationship
- Experiences you may have missed out on

Your grief is going to be layered—and that's okay. Instead of judging yourself or trying to understand or make sense of this grief, just try to hold space for these feelings. You'll find that, with time, this grief will ease up and feel less overwhelming. Below are four different activities you can do to facilitate your grieving process:

- **Goodbye Letter:** Write a goodbye letter to the person or thing that you are grieving (that you will not send). In this letter, be honest and share all your thoughts and feelings.

- **Grieving Time:** Make space for your grief by setting aside fifteen to twenty minutes a day to cry and just sit with these feelings of grief. Feel free to journal or write down any thoughts or feelings that arise.

- **Create Meaning:** Find meaning in other aspects of your life by connecting with loved ones and reengaging in activities that bring you joy or offer you a sense of peace.

Exercise: Settle Your Nervous System

Despite the trauma you have experienced and the grief you might endure, your mind and body are resilient and have the ability to heal. Part of this healing process involves stabilizing your overactive nervous system. You can do this through grounding and self-soothing techniques. Think of these techniques as tools that can help you calm your body and regulate your emotions when you are in distress. In this visualization exercise, adapted from the EMDR protocol developed by Francine Shapiro and tapping exercise by Laurel Parnell, you will have the opportunity to develop and practice a self-soothing technique you can use on your own at any time. Simply follow the prompts below.

Please note: If this exercise at any point causes you distress or brings up any negative feelings, memories, or sensations, discontinue immediately. It's important to listen to your body and take cues. It's okay if you need to ease into this healing process and do it at a pace that feels right for you. You can always return to this exercise in the future.

1. Think of a real or imaginary place you can visit in your mind where you feel calm, comfortable, and relaxed. This place can be somewhere you have been before, have seen in a movie or picture, or someplace you have completely made up. Keep in mind that this place should not be associated with any upsetting or disturbing memories or experiences.

    Example: *A private beach somewhere tropical.*

2. Once you have identified this place, picture yourself there and connect to your five senses. What do you see? Hear? Taste? Smell? Touch?

   Example: *You're standing on the shoreline. You are barefoot with your toes gently pressing into the sand, the water grazing your ankles. It's warm and there is a soft breeze. You can smell and taste the saltiness of the ocean and feel the sun beaming on your skin. You hear the sounds of the waves rolling in.*

3. Now, notice how you are feeling while visualizing and connecting to this peaceful place. Consider your emotions and the sensations you may be experiencing in your body. If you feel generally good and calm, notice that and allow yourself to enjoy these feelings.

   Example: *You notice yourself feeling pretty relaxed and less anxious. You notice the tension in your shoulders start to dissipate and your heart rate starts to slow down.*

4. Next, to further enhance and connect to this feeling state, try to add some *very slow* tapping. Alternate tapping back and forth about six to ten times.

   Option 1: Cross your arms, giving yourself a butterfly hug, and very slowly alternate tapping your right and left shoulder back and forth.

   Option 2: Lay your hands gently on your knees and slowly alternate tapping your left and right knee back and forth.

5. After this first round of tapping, pause and identify a positive cue word or phrase to associate with this place you have visualized (i.e., "Peace, "My safe place," "Comfort"). Say this word in your head or out loud while bringing up the same picture or image and do another slow round of tapping.

6. Finally, you are going to test this cue word. First, focus your attention on something that's only minorly annoying (i.e., a

car alarm going off, stubbing your toe) and observe how you feel or how your body responds to this minor annoyance. Then, say your cue word or phrase and bring your calm place back to mind, focusing again on your senses and how it feels in your body. Conclude this visualization with at least one more slow round of tapping.

Try practicing this visualization exercise daily when you are already in a calm and relaxed state. Like any other skill, if you practice regularly, you will feel more confident in your ability to access and use this skill in the future when you really need it. It will feel more natural and accessible to you, even during those more difficult times when you are feeling dysregulated or experiencing heightened anxiety (Parnell 2008, 48).

Let's Recap

Emotionally abusive relationships are traumatic and can be considered a form of complex trauma. Therefore, you are likely to experience trauma responses post abuse because of the changes that occur at a molecular level. In addition to trauma, you will also be confronted with feelings of grief. This grief will probably be layered and reflect the many losses you experience after ending your relationship with the EAP. While these aftereffects can be overwhelming, you are resilient and can overcome them. Fortunately, your mind and body have the capacity to heal. This healing involves honoring your feelings, continuing to practice self-compassion, and developing techniques to calm and stabilize your nervous system.

Chapter 7

Challenging Your Negative Core Beliefs

Coming out of an emotionally abusive relationship can be disorienting. When you have been immersed in the world of an EAP—constantly questioning and doubting yourself, adjusting or changing your behaviors to meet the unrealistic expectations and needs of your partner, and submitting yourself to this false reality out of survival—your sense of self and belief system becomes skewed. It can almost feel as if you have been brainwashed and now need to deprogram yourself—challenging the negative core beliefs you have internalized and come to believe as being true.

In this chapter, you will learn about common negative core beliefs that many individuals recovering from emotionally abusive relationships internalize. You will also become familiar with some of the unhelpful thinking habits you might be regularly engaging in that are hindering you from fully recovering from the trauma of the abuse. You will then have the opportunity to develop strategies that will help you challenge these problematic beliefs and thinking habits and cultivate more positive and adaptive beliefs to increase your sense of self-worth and self-empowerment. I recognize that this process can feel overwhelming and stir up other unpleasant emotions, but when you are able to single out these negative core beliefs and see them for what they are—a product of your abuse—it becomes easier to disentangle yourself from these beliefs that continue to linger even after the relationship is long over.

Identifying Negative Core Beliefs

The beliefs and narratives we come to form about ourselves, our relationships with others, and the world are largely influenced by life events and our attachments. So, when you have been in an emotionally abusive relationship, your core beliefs often reflect this experience. Sometimes, your beliefs reflect the language or mimic the words of your abuser. Other times, your beliefs are formed from your interpretation or understanding of your experiences in the relationship. There's also the possibility that some of your negative core beliefs are the outcome of other significant events, relationships in your life, or other outside influences (which we will discuss in greater detail in chapter 8). For example, if you experienced childhood abuse, sexual assault, or lived through a natural disaster, you might have come to develop the belief "I'm not safe" or "I'm powerless." These beliefs can then be further reinforced and strengthened by your emotionally abusive relationship.

Our negative core beliefs are fundamentally flawed beliefs we have come to internalize about ourselves and who we are. They are inaccurate, unkind, and unhelpful—yet, it can be difficult for us to see them as such. These beliefs typically fall into one of these four themes: defectiveness, responsibility, vulnerability, and lack of control (Shapiro 2018). Read through these four themes and some of the common beliefs and consider which resonate most.

Beliefs of Defectiveness

• Joanna's Story

Joanna had started therapy because she was struggling in a new relationship. Although she had been divorced from her EAP for a few years, she continued to maintain the belief "I'm selfish." Her ex had called her "selfish" on multiple occasions. He was particularly keen on calling her selfish for pursuing her doctorate and career goals. He didn't like when she would study or be unable to attend a social event because of her schoolwork or other school-related obligations.

Now, in this new relationship, Joanna was constantly worried about being perceived as selfish and was consistently putting her needs second to those of her current partner. She started to pay for most things, cancel her own plans to accommodate her partner's schedule, and limit the time she spent with her friends. This belief that she was selfish made it difficult for her to live a life that reflected her own values and honored her own needs.

A core belief of defectiveness is when you maintain the belief that there is something inherently "wrong" with you. Examples of this type of core belief:

- "I'm not good enough."
- "I'm bad."
- "I'm insignificant."
- "I'm crazy."
- "I can't do anything right."
- "I'm not lovable."

When you believe that there is something wrong with you or that *your existence* is wrong, you tend to be overly critical of yourself and put yourself down. You also tend to try and prove yourself to others and people-please. You also may find yourself being more tolerant of unkind and disrespectful behavior. So, when you treat yourself poorly, it doesn't faze you as much when others do—and can make you more vulnerable to emotionally abusive partners.

Beliefs of Responsibility

• Cody's Story

Cody had been in both an emotionally and a physically abusive relationship for close to two years before he left. Initially, his partner was very kind and loving and it felt so easy. They seemed to have a lot in common and could relate to one another on a deeper level—both having experienced childhood trauma and having struggled with their mental health. Cody had been on cloud nine—he had never felt as seen or had been as close to anyone. Unfortunately, over time, Cody's partner became aggressive and violent. First, verbally, and then, physically. It continued to escalate over the course of their relationship before Cody finally left him.

Cody blamed himself for almost everything that occurred within the relationship. He blamed himself for the abuse and would obsess over the times he had said the "wrong thing" or "upset" his partner. He blamed himself for not seeing the red flags or being able to detect the coercion and controlling behaviors earlier on. He blamed himself for how long he stayed, maintaining the belief that he should have left when his partner started to become emotionally abusive. This self-blame persisted post abuse, becoming a theme in other areas of his life, including in his work and non-romantic relationships.

A core belief of responsibility is when you maintain a belief that you are at fault or responsible for an event or series of events. Examples of this type of core belief:

- "It's my fault."
- "I should have known better."
- "I did something wrong."
- "I could have done something differently."
- "I can't be trusted."

When you take full responsibility and blame for things that are outside of your control or influence, you become more vulnerable to feelings of guilt and shame and are more likely to take responsibility for things you are not responsible for or at least fully responsible for. These beliefs can make you feel as though you deserve abusive or unkind behavior or can become a means of excusing these types of behaviors in your relationships.

Beliefs of Vulnerability

- ### Dani's Story

    Dani initiated therapy because she was having a difficult time dating after her breakup with her emotionally abusive partner. When they first met, Dani's partner had been quite charming. He planned elaborate dates and would always compliment her and tell her how much he liked her. He talked a lot about their future and the life he wanted to build with her. Initially, Dani was put off by this behavior. While it was nice to date someone who was so direct and open about their feelings and intentions, it also felt a little too intense. She wondered if this person and relationship were too good to be true.

    A year into their relationship, Dani's partner was noticeably different. He stopped initiating dates and would give Dani a hard time when she would suggest that they go out to dinner or do something fun outside the home—calling her a "princess" or "ungrateful" for asking for more. He switched from being complimentary to being hypercritical of her. He also became increasingly possessive of her and would give her a hard time for wanting occasional alone time or when she would make plans with her friends.

    When Dani eventually ended the relationship, she was mostly angry at herself. In therapy, Dani reflected on the red flags she missed and the things that had made her uncomfortable. She was mad at herself for her "poor judgment" and not listening to her gut.

She felt vulnerable dating and was worried that she would never be able to fully trust herself and her judgment moving forward.

A core belief of vulnerability is when you hold the belief that you are unsafe or vulnerable even when there is no current or present threat. Examples of this type of core belief:

- "I am unsafe."
- "All men are unsafe."
- "I can't trust men/women."
- "I can't trust anyone."
- "I can't trust myself."
- "I can't trust my judgment."

When you cling to the belief that you are perpetually vulnerable or unsafe, it can result in self-isolation and perpetuate feelings of mistrust in others and the world at large. Therefore, in this attempt to protect yourself, you may unintentionally reinforce this unhelpful belief.

Beliefs of Lack of Control

• Rachel's Story

Rachel had been married to her husband for over twenty years and initiated therapy because she had been contemplating ending the marriage. She gave example after example of different occasions her husband had minimized and invalidated her feelings and put her down. While she was able to see the damage this relationship had caused her and the impact it had on her mental health and self-worth, she firmly held the belief that she was stuck and it was her destiny to stay in this relationship. She believed she had to sacrifice her own happiness for the sake of her marriage and family.

A core belief of lack of control is when you overgeneralize your lack of control or agency and maintain the belief that you're completely helpless. Examples of this type of core belief:

- "I have no control."
- "I am helpless."
- "I cannot get what I want."
- "I am powerless."
- "I cannot succeed."

When you are convinced that you don't have any power or control over your life, it can feel easier to just submit to your circumstances. However, this sense of powerlessness can make it difficult to leave situations that are harmful and unsafe.

Exercise: Pause and Reflect

Take a moment to explore your own negative core beliefs. What are some of the things you consistently tell yourself that are self-limiting or harmful? If you are having a difficult time identifying a specific belief, go through the four different themes: defectiveness, responsibility, vulnerability, and lack of control. Consider the origins of these beliefs, their legitimacy, and the impact they have had on your day-to-day life and inner experience. Maybe try to imagine how it would feel to be free of these beliefs.

Bringing Awareness to Harmful Thinking Patterns

The negative core beliefs that become crystalized in our minds play into how we perceive and respond to events and stressors. While these cognitive distortions develop as a means of self-protection, these automatic, fear-based responses can become detrimental. For example, if you hold the belief "I'm not good enough," you won't see yourself accurately and will engage in thinking patterns that both reflect and maintain this belief. Part of your deprogramming requires identifying and then challenging these harmful thinking patterns you have become accustomed to and learning to become more flexible in your thinking. Below, I've listed the different types of cognitive distortions you may be vulnerable to. As you read, pay attention to the negative core beliefs you see yourself engaging in. Later in the chapter, you will learn skills for unlearning these unhelpful thinking patterns so you can start to live a more authentic, fulfilling life.

Black-and-White Thinking: Black-and-white thinking is when you think in the binary or in terms of "either, or." As a result, you fall into the habit of categorizing things as being "good or bad" or "wrong or right." Your mind doesn't typically consider the "gray" because everything falls into only one of two categories.

Example: *When you tell yourself you're a "bad friend" for forgetting to call your best friend on their birthday because you reason that "a good friend would never forget" versus recognizing that you have had a lot on your plate and made an honest, human mistake.*

Overgeneralization: Overgeneralization is when you use evidence from a single experience and apply it to all future experiences. You make a rule or a general assumption based on one or a few events.

Example: *When you go on a couple of bad dates and tell yourself, "Dating is terrible and a waste of my time" versus acknowledging that part of dating involves not-so-great dates and a variety of experiences.*

Catastrophizing: Catastrophizing is the habit of predicting the worst-case scenario or outcome with limited to no supporting evidence or facts.

Example: *You finally left your abusive partner and tell yourself, "Nobody will ever want me because I am divorced with kids and have all this baggage, so I'll probably just die alone" versus considering that there are plenty of other divorced, single parents in the world also seeking connection.*

Mental Filtering: Mental filtering occurs when you filter out or minimize the good or positive aspects of an experience (or don't recognize them at all) and focus solely on the negative.

Example: *When you start to date someone new and it's going well, but you start fixating on some of the trivial differences and tell yourself, "We have different tastes in music" or "They don't like the same food" instead of acknowledging all the positive aspects of this new relationship, such as shared values, feeling safe, and enjoying one another's company.*

Emotional Reasoning: Emotional reasoning is when you come to a conclusion or make an assumption based on how you feel versus actual facts or concrete evidence. Therefore, your thoughts reflect how you are feeling or your current affective state.

Example: *When you feel uneasy or anxious at a social gathering and tell yourself, "Everyone is judging me" or "Nobody wants me here," but do not have actual proof of this to be true.*

Labeling: Labeling occurs when you define yourself or others based on a single behavior or action. Basically, you globalize a single instance or situation as a defining characteristic—typically, a flaw.

Example: *When you spill something on yourself or notice a stain on your shirt and then tell yourself, "God, I'm such a slob!"*

Our thoughts and how we talk to ourselves matter and can make or break our mental health and sense of self-worth. Next, we will discuss different techniques and strategies to help you break free from these thinking patterns that could inadvertently make it difficult for you to fully heal.

Challenging Negative Core Beliefs and Unhelpful Thinking Habits

Identifying your negative core beliefs and unhelpful thinking habits is half the battle. This is because our thoughts often occur automatically and outside our conscious awareness—especially after trauma or when we have been engaging in certain ways of thinking for years or (in many cases) for most of our lives. Therefore, challenging these thoughts and beliefs requires a conscious effort. The strategies below are evidence-based and can help you start this process of disentangling yourself from these cognitive distortions.

Diffuse Your Thoughts

Most of us engage with our thoughts rather carelessly. They just pop up and we engage with them as if they were truths or facts. However, as discussed, our thoughts are often inaccurate and a result of our experiences, including trauma. Thought diffusion is a mindful practice that helps us create distance from our thoughts so we are not as affected by them (Harris 2008). For instance, if you find yourself thinking, *I will never have a healthy relationship,* imagine trying these different techniques to diffuse yourself from this inaccurate and unhelpful thought.

Call it out. Tell yourself, "I'm having the thought that _____" or "My trauma brain is telling me _____." When we call out our thought for what it is—simply a thought or an idea—we are less likely to fuse to it or experience an emotional response.

Poke fun at it. Instead of ruminating over a thought or getting caught up in a thought loop, sing or belt it out or say it to yourself in a silly voice or character (i.e., think Kermit the Frog).

Journal. Another great way of diffusing yourself from a thought is to write it down. By externalizing it and seeing the thought as a string of words or letters, it loses its meaning and weight.

Deconstruct Your Thoughts

Again, a lot of our thoughts and beliefs are rooted in past experiences. When we can deconstruct our thoughts and identify their origins, as well as triggers or situations that activate us, it makes it easier to more objectively see and respond to our thoughts so they loosen their grip. Below, I've outlined the steps you can take to deconstruct your thoughts. You'll notice that when you approach your thoughts with more curiosity and less judgment, they become easier to tolerate and manage.

1. **Identify the intrusive/upsetting thought.**

   Example: "*I am not in control.*"

2. **Identify the feelings that are activated.**

   Example: "*I'm anxious, scared.*"

3. **Notice where you are experiencing these feelings in your body.**

   Example: "*My chest.*"

4. **Identify instances in your relationship in which these feelings came up.**

   Example: "*When my ex would give me the silent treatment for days at a time.*"

5. **Identify the various situations that trigger this thought and feeling state.**

   Example: "*When I don't hear back from someone*" or "*When my coworker is moody.*"

6. **Consider an alternative, more accurate, and helpful thought for this present situation.**

   Example: "*I have choices,*" "*I am strong,*" "*I am not in that situation anymore.*"

As previously discussed, like all new skills, these techniques require practice. The more you practice and apply them, the more they become second nature and easy to mentally access when you are experiencing an intrusive thought or spiraling. Try setting aside some time each day to take inventory of your thoughts and practice using some of these strategies to challenge those thoughts that are harmful or unhelpful. I recommend using a journal to log this process by including the cognitive distortions you're noticing and the reframe or alternative thoughts you come up with.

Integrating Positive Core Beliefs

Another technique to support your deprogramming is to integrate and strengthen more positive and helpful core beliefs—beliefs that encourage positive emotions and well-being. You can do this by connecting to memories and past experiences that reinforce these beliefs and elicit a more desired feeling state (i.e., confidence, calm, safety).

Exercise: Reinforcing Positive Beliefs

In this next visualization exercise, you will have the opportunity to practice and develop this technique. Similar to the EMDR exercise in chapter 6, in this next exercise adapted from the work of Francine Shapiro, you will use bilateral stimulation (tapping) to enhance your experience, including the positive feelings and sensations that are likely to arise. Simply follow the prompts below.

Please note: If this exercise at any point causes you distress or brings up any negative feelings, memories, or sensations, discontinue immediately. It's important to listen to your body and take cues. It's okay if you need to ease into this healing process and do it at a pace that feels right for you. You can always return to this exercise in the future.

1. Identify the negative core belief you are working to challenge or dismantle.

   Example: *"I'm not good enough."*

2. Identify an alternative, positive core belief to replace this negative core belief. You can do this by asking yourself, *"What would I prefer to believe about myself?"*

   Example: *"I am okay as I am."*

3. Next, identify a past moment, memory, or experience in your life when you were able to fully connect to this positive core belief or knew this belief to be true.

   Example: *"My sixteenth birthday with my two best friends."*

4. Now, bring up an image of this moment. Picture yourself there and connect to your five senses. What do you see? Hear? Taste? Smell? Touch?

   Example: *You're in your childhood bedroom with your friends, wearing your favorite pajamas. You are all laughing, eating pizza, and watching your favorite rom-com.*

5. Now, notice how you feel while visualizing and connecting to this specific moment. What emotions are you feeling? How does your body feel?

   Example: *You notice yourself feeling more comfortable and relaxed in your body. You notice yourself smiling. You feel loved and accepted.*

6. Next, to further enhance and connect to this moment in time, try to add some *very slow* tapping. Alternate tapping back and forth six to ten times.

   Option 1: Cross your arms, giving yourself a butterfly hug, and very slowly alternate tapping your right and left shoulder back and forth.

   Option 2: Lay your hands gently on your knees and slowly alternate tapping your left and right knee back and forth.

7. After tapping, pause and identify a positive cue word or phrase to associate with this moment. Say this word or phrase in your head or out loud while bringing up the same picture or image and do two or three more rounds of slow tapping.

Try practicing this technique daily and with various positive core beliefs you want to strengthen and feel more connected to (Shapiro 2018, 249).

Let's Recap

Emotionally abusive relationships can cause deep wounds—and their effects can be lasting. You have likely internalized negative beliefs and narratives from the trauma you experienced. However, you are resilient and have the capacity to heal. Your brain is malleable, and when you can identify these cognitive distortions and actively challenge these self-limiting beliefs and thinking habits using the strategies discussed, you further release yourself from the past and the grip of the EAP. Through this deprogramming, you'll be able to see yourself more accurately, reconnect to your authentic self, and have a stronger sense of self-worth.

Chapter 8

Taking Time to Heal

Life post abuse can be overwhelming, and the healing process daunting. It's hard to go back to business as usual after being in the throes of an emotionally abusive relationship. You might be asking yourself, "Will I ever recover from this?" Or maybe you're googling, "How to move on from an abusive relationship." There are often feelings of restlessness and a desire to "get over it." However, I'm sorry to say, there is no quick fix or magic wand. Healing from an emotionally abusive relationship is going to take time, patience, and commitment—but it *is* possible, and you can and *will* get there.

In this chapter, you will be asked to go a little bit deeper and consider how past experiences and/or unhealed trauma and attachment wounds may have made you more vulnerable to the abuse you endured. You will also learn about and explore the role of social conditioning, how internalized social constructs and norms may also have influenced you, and how you have come to understand and navigate relationships. This self-exploration is crucial to your healing because it will help you gain greater insight into your patterns of behavior and beliefs, as well as help you develop even greater self-compassion.

Exploring Your Past

If you were to be prompted, "Tell me about your childhood," how might you feel or respond? Would you shy away? Would you be reluctant? Would you feel overwhelmed? Maybe you would respond with, "I don't have any trauma," "My childhood was fine," or "I don't really want to talk about the past." This is understandable: doing this kind of self-reflection often requires more vulnerability and, more often than not, more work. However, while it is tempting to avoid the past because it feels too painful or seems "insignificant" or "irrelevant" to the present, I promise you that it can be quite healing and empowering to understand where you came from and why you do the things you do. But before diving deep, let's start with the very basics to help you understand how your past informs your present.

Your Family of Origin

Take a moment and consider some of your quirks—those things you do that maybe most of your friends or loved ones don't. These quirks or idiosyncrasies are the things you do out of habit, that you probably never think twice about. Maybe it's how you fold your laundry or some of your go-to phrases. Maybe it's a very specific food preference or an odd phobia. Maybe it's a very rigid morning routine or the way you organize your office supplies. What are *your* quirks?

Now, consider where these quirks came from. Chances are at least some of these quirks are learned behaviors that you observed in your family and environment during childhood—this is where a lot of our behavioral patterns take form. Maybe you use some of the same language as your mom, have similar mannerisms, or have a very similar sense of humor (that doesn't always land). How we were raised and the environment we were raised in greatly influences how we behave, think, emote, communicate, respond to stressors, and navigate relationships. During childhood, we absorb everything. We look to our parents or caregivers as all-knowing authority figures. We trust that the adults in our lives—these wise people with much more life under their belt—have all the answers and that their way is *the* right way. So, we mimic and mirror their behaviors and internalize many of their beliefs—which then can manifest in our adult lives and relationships.

Learned Self-Talk

Another example of a learned behavior is our self-talk. "Self-talk" is the way we speak to ourselves, the things we say to ourselves—both in our head and out loud. Sometimes, our self-talk is kind; other times, it's critical. And a lot of our self-talk reflects what we experienced and observed during our childhood. For instance, if you are self-critical of your appearance and body image, there is a good chance that your negative self-talk reflects the self-talk of your parent or primary caregiver(s) (and, maybe, even your parent's parent). Examples of this negative self-talk might include: "I can't leave the house looking like this," "I look too old," "I need to lose weight," "I hate my thighs," "I look terrible in this."

It's important to consider your self-talk: how you speak to yourself directly impacts your self-esteem and self-confidence and how you see yourself in the context of your relationships. Additionally, when you are able to identify the root of your self-talk and have a clearer understanding of where some of these negative self-talk statements come from, you'll find it easier to challenge or replace these negative statements with positive self-talk statements that are more encouraging and supportive. Sometimes these learned behaviors can be helpful and adaptive; other times, they can be disadvantageous.

Exercise: Pause and Reflect

Take a moment to reflect on your own self-talk. Get curious. Where did these self-talk statements come from? Were any of these statements learned or role-modeled? Or perhaps your self-talk is a direct result of emotional abuse by a parent or family member (we will get more into this in a bit). Again, there is a high likelihood that some of these statements may have been passed down to you in some form or another by a parent or family member.

Journal prompt: List as many of your self-talk statements as possible (both positive and negative). With this list, go through each statement one by one and write down the origins of these statements (i.e., "This is something my mom always told herself," "My dad always called himself 'Idiot'").

Internalizing Negative Feedback

Of course, we are also impacted by how we were parented and how the other family members in our young lives engaged with us and spoke to us. For example, if your parents were hypercritical of you or had ridiculously high expectations of you, you may have internalized some of these criticisms or taken on these expectations yourself. Or, if your parents regularly minimized or invalidated your feelings and experiences, you likely question or doubt your feelings and experiences in your adult life. The feedback we received from the people closest to us has a significant impact on our self-concept and sense of self-worth. Here are some examples of both negative and positive feedback:

Examples of negative feedback:

- Your parent labeling you as "too sensitive," "dramatic," or "immature."

- When crying/upset, your parents responded with, "It's not that big of a deal" or "You shouldn't be so upset."

- Being regularly teased by your siblings about your weight.

- Your parents comparing you to your high-achieving sibling.

- Being yelled at or taunted by your parent every time you make a mistake.

Examples of positive feedback:

- Your older sibling being protective of you.

- Your parent regularly encouraging you and telling you, "You can do anything you put your mind to."

- Your parent coming to every one of your sports games and always expressing support of your goals and ambitions.
- Your parent providing you with emotional support and validation when you are going through a difficult time.
- Your grandparent telling you how proud they are of you.

Exercise: Pause and Reflect

Take a moment to consider your childhood and upbringing, and the feedback you received from your parent(s) and/or other family members in your life. Was it positive? Negative? Or maybe you experienced a bit of both. How did this feedback impact you? Did this feedback harm or help your confidence and sense of self-worth?

The Relationships You Observed

When reflecting on our family of origin, it's also important to consider the types of relationships we were around—these relationships often become our template of what we think a relationship "looks like" or how it "should" be. If you observed a caring, mutually respectful relationship between your parents, chances are you will expect and seek out a similar partnership. On the flip side, if you witnessed two adults barely tolerating one another or one berating the other, this may become the norm or something that just "is." It does not mean that you necessarily strive for an unhealthy or unhappy relationship, but these relationships can normalize certain dynamics or shape your expectations—with the bar being set lower than what you actually may want *and* deserve.

Here are some examples of relationship dynamics or patterns you may have observed or learned from:

- Being part of a culture or family that normalizes cheating and infidelity

- Having parents who have been openly unhappy with one another, yet have stayed together for various reasons, including religious beliefs, financial security, or the stigma of divorce

- Observing your parents regularly scream at each other and criticize one another

- Witnessing domestic violence or other forms of abuse between your parents

- Your parent regularly confiding in you about their negative feelings toward the other parent

When you grow up around relationships that are imbalanced or abusive, it can be difficult to discriminate "normal" from healthy. Therefore, what may be "normal" to you may not be healthy or reflective of what you deserve in a partner or relationship. Many people reenact their parents' relationship in their own, not knowing that they have the right to something better that makes them feel safe, respected, and cared for. Below are some examples of how these influences might manifest in your own romantic relationships and dating life:

- Gravitating toward turbulent relationships because you have come to associate romantic relationships with chaos and conflict and/or believe that regular fighting and dysfunction are part of every relationship

- Mistaking high-stress and volatile relationships with "passion" and romanticizing abusive behaviors (which was discussed in chapter 4)

- Experiencing feelings of familiarity and comfort when in an abusive dynamic

- Interpreting certain healthy behaviors and qualities in a partner or prospective partner (i.e., easygoing, communicative of their feelings, consistent) as being "boring"

- Losing interest quickly in stable relationships because you are accustomed to partners who are hot and cold or unpredictable

This is why exploring your past and backstory matters. It can clue you in as to why you are the way you are and why you engage in some of the behaviors you engage in in your adult relationships—including why you might have tolerated the abusive behavior of the EAP for as long as you did.

Exercise: Pause and Reflect

Take a moment to consider the relationships you observed during childhood. Were these relationships loving and supportive, or were they openly nasty and hostile? Did your parents or adult family members seem happy in their relationship or unhappy? Did the relationships seem healthy or unhealthy? Get curious and think about how these relationships may have impacted you and if they have influenced your preferences or behaviors when it comes to your own romantic relationships.

Journal prompt: What are the things you liked and/or did not like about your parents' relationship or the other adult relationships you observed growing up? What are some of the things you can learn from these relationships that motivate you to do things differently moving forward?

Attachment Trauma and Your Attachment Style

- ### Lana's Story

    Lana had been in two consecutive, long-term relationships with emotionally abusive partners. After ending her most recent relationship, she felt desperate. How was it possible that she ended up in another abusive relationship? "What is wrong with me?" Lana asked herself. Seeking answers, Lana initiated therapy.

    At first, Lana resisted talking about her childhood. She didn't think it was relevant or necessary. However, as she became more comfortable in therapy, Lana started to reflect on and open up about her relationship with her parents. Lana was an only child. Her parents were "workaholics" and she was primarily raised by her nanny. When her parents were around, Lana described them as being emotionally distant. They were rarely affectionate and didn't seem too interested in her life or extracurricular activities. She knew, logically, that they loved her—but there was a part of her that believed she was unlovable.

As she further explored her childhood experiences and reflected on memories with her parents, Lana started to gain a better understanding of herself and was able to identify one of her negative core beliefs: "I am unlovable." This core belief had been damaging and, over the course of her life, compromised her sense of self-worth and self-esteem. As a result, she was more tolerant of unkind and abusive behaviors from partners and the men she dated.

As you know now, some experiences that might not seem "traumatic" can have a profound impact on your core beliefs, your sense of self-worth, and the relationships you gravitate toward. This includes attachment trauma. Attachment trauma can be understood as a series of experiences or set of circumstances in your interpersonal relationships that pose a threat to your sense of safety and of being loved. Unfortunately, these experiences are often normalized and minimized.

Examples of attachment trauma include:

- Parent/child separation (i.e., divorce, death of a parent)

- Family difficulties (i.e., financial hardship, homelessness, a parent with untreated addiction or mental illness)

- Childhood abuse (physical, emotional, sexual)

- Childhood neglect (emotional and physical)

- Witnessing violence or abuse in the home

- Bullying and alienation (by peers, family, or authority figures)

In this next exercise, you will have an opportunity to explore and identify one of these stressful or upsetting experiences.

Exercise: Getting to the Root of It

1. Think about your emotionally abusive relationship and identify a specific moment or incident that was particularly activating or upsetting.

   Example: *Moment: "When my ex berated me at a restaurant and called me a slob because I spilled water on the table."*

2. Next, identify the feelings that come up for you when you think of this memory and notice where you are experiencing these feelings in your body.

   Example: *Feelings: Shame, embarrassed, insecure. Body sensations: tightness in my chest, palms are sweaty.*

3. Now, close your eyes, and allow your mind to float back to your past. Consider when you first felt this way or if there is a specific event or incident linked to this feeling and negative core belief.

   Example: *"When my mom would yell at me for forgetting my lunch at home."*

4. With this specific event or incident in mind, consider how this experience impacted you and the negative core beliefs that may have been deep-seated or reinforced by this experience. (Tip: Go back and reference chapter 7 to help you identify this belief.)

   Example: *Impact: I felt like I was a burden and that I was always disappointing my mom. Negative core belief: I'm not good enough.*

When you can get to the root of your negative core beliefs, they become easier to dispute and challenge. You are also likely to show yourself more compassion because you recognize that these thoughts are the product of unhealed attachment wounds.

Attachment trauma is especially impactful because, as discussed in chapter 2, when these experiences go unaddressed or unhealed, they can negatively impact your attachment style. As a quick refresher, attachment is the experience of how you emotionally connect and relate to others. Your attachment style is largely informed by childhood experiences and how you bonded (or did not bond) with your caregivers, as well as the quality of your peer relationships and other significant relationships throughout your life.

Your attachment style influences your ability to trust others, have meaningful relationships, and your general sense of self-worth. Therefore, when you experience safe and positive relationships during childhood, you tend to do well in your adult relationships and are capable of emotional intimacy. Alternatively, if you experienced abuse, neglect, or ostracism during childhood, you can really struggle in your interpersonal relationships, leading to an avoidant, anxious attachment style or disorganized attachment style—attachment styles that can put you at greater risk of being more vulnerable to unhealthy or unsafe people and relationships in your adult life.

Below, I have defined four distinct attachment styles. These attachment styles are classified by a set pattern of behavior and indicate how one typically navigates relationships and intimacy. Read through them and, without judgment, consider which of these attachment styles most resonates with you.

Secure Attachment: When you have a secure attachment style, you find value in your relationships, while also appreciating your independence. You generally have high self-esteem and feel secure in yourself and in your relationships. You feel comfortable communicating your feelings, welcome closeness and intimacy, and tend to be trusting of others (including your romantic partners). You are also good at providing validation to your partner if they struggle with their own insecurities or have an insecure attachment, while also having limits that protect your autonomy, mental health, and overall well-being.

Anxious Attachment: When you have an anxious attachment style, you experience a persistent fear of abandonment or rejection. You are typically clingy in your relationships and hypersensitive to any change in behavior that might suggest another person is going to leave or end the relationship. Other behaviors you may exhibit include worrying about being liked or feelings not being reciprocated, becoming emotionally dysregulated when you detect any form of rejection, and seeking regular validation from your partner. You may also struggle with feeling worthy and go above and beyond to change or morph yourself into being the type of person you think your partner or other people want you to be.

Avoidant Attachment: When you have an avoidant attachment style, you tend to fear closeness and intimacy with others, as well as resist relying on another person—especially your partner. If you are avoidant, you have hesitation around commitment and are often ambivalent about your relationships. You tend to push others away and crave independence. Other patterns of behavior that are common in individuals with an avoidant attachment style include challenges with emotional expression, being emotionally unavailable, and regularly seeking space or withdrawing from relationships completely (Levine and Heller 2011).

Disorganized Attachment: When you have a disorganized attachment style, you both desire and crave intimacy and connection and also fear these things. You struggle with trust and tend to oscillate between feeling anxious and insecure in your relationships and avoiding relationships completely. Common behaviors for individuals with a disorganized attachment style include high emotionality, being untrusting of others, and exhibiting erratic behavior in relationships (Paetzold et al. 2015).

When you gain insight into your attachment style, you'll have more context to work with to both understand and combat some of your thinking habits and behaviors that may have made you more susceptible to the abuse you endured. For example, if you come to determine that you have an anxious attachment style, you might recognize that your deep-rooted fear of abandonment made you more tolerant of the EAP's abusive behaviors. When you are worried about being left or abandoned by your partner, you might go to great lengths to keep your partner happy and appease them. Or, if you have a disorganized attachment style, you might feel most comfortable in turbulent relationships because these are the relationships you are most familiar with and know best.

Exercise: Pause and Reflect

Take a moment to reflect on your relationships and interpersonal experiences during your childhood and more formative years of your life. How have these relationships and experiences shaped you and your attachment style? Do you have a difficult time trusting or being vulnerable with others? Do you struggle with your self-esteem and sense of worthiness? Give yourself time to process these experiences and honor any feelings that come up.

Exploring Social Influence and Conditioning

• Catherine's Story

Catherine had been married to her husband for ten years prior to them separating. She had been introduced to her husband through her church at age eighteen and they married when she was twenty. Before they married, Catherine's ex had been very kind and respectful. After they married, things changed. Catherine's husband became extremely controlling. He wouldn't let her spend time outside the home or with her friends alone. He also discouraged her from getting a job after college because he believed that her working would interfere with her duties and responsibilities as his wife. When Catherine and her husband had kids, her husband's behavior only escalated. Her husband became more and more aggressive toward her, calling her names and constantly criticizing her and her housework. Catherine had been contemplating ending her relationship for a while. She didn't want to continue living the life she was living and have her kids exposed to the abuse. Finally, after almost ten years of marriage, Catherine left.

As Catherine began to process the abuse in therapy, she came to realize that the reason she had stayed as long as she did was because of the expectations of her church community and some of the religious values and constructs she had internalized. She had been raised to believe that her role as a wife was to serve her husband. Now, as an adult and mother, Catherine started to understand that these values and norms did not reflect her personal values and what she wanted for herself and her children. Catherine wanted to be in a loving relationship that was built on mutual respect. She wanted to be an equal with her partner and have a relationship that was supportive of her autonomy and personal ambitions.

Thus, in addition to your upbringing, family of origin, and attachment trauma, it's important to consider how your social conditioning may have contributed to your understanding of romantic relationships and your response to the emotional abuse that you experienced. Social conditioning is the experience of taking on the beliefs, values, and norms of one's social group as your own. Social conditioning starts during childhood and is largely influenced by your family culture, religion or religious upbringing, formal education and schooling, peer relationships, and media—and it continues throughout adulthood.

Social conditioning influences your expectations of other people's behavior and what you deem as being "acceptable" or "normal" behavior (Stewart et al. 2021). Below are some examples of how social conditioning can inform your beliefs about relationships and response to abusive behavior:

- Tolerating or rationalizing your male partner's problematic behavior because you have been socialized to believe "women are just emotional" and/or "boys will be boys."

- Staying in an abusive dynamic because you have been conditioned to believe that all relationships are hard and require work.

- Being reluctant to initiate divorce or separation with an abusive partner because your religious organization discourages or condemns divorce.

- Submitting to your abusive partner because you have been taught by your religion that your role is to submit to your male spouse.

- Fearing leaving an abusive relationship due to seeing your peers or other members of your community being ostracized for being single.

Social conditioning can often generate feelings of helplessness. When you internalize social norms and constructs that are disempowering, it can make it difficult to feel like you have any real control or agency over your life. The good news is you can unlearn all of these things and start to work toward living more authentically and in a way that is more in alignment with your personal values and beliefs.

Exercise: Pause and Reflect

Take a moment to consider how your social conditioning may have informed your beliefs about relationships and how you perceived and responded to the abuse. What are some of the social norms or constructs that have been disempowering or have made you question yourself and your judgment about your relationship?

Let's Recap

While you might shy away from going deep and doing the inner work, remember, it's imperative to your healing. Understanding the origins of your negative self-talk; attachment style; and internalized social norms, beliefs, and values can help you understand why you may have been more vulnerable to the abuse you endured, as well as why it may have been difficult for you to leave. Remember, knowledge is power. And when you do the work to get to know and understand yourself, it can empower you to take your life back and create a life that reflects what *you* want and what is important to *you*.

Chapter 9

Finding Empowerment

When you are in an emotionally abusive relationship, your whole life revolves around your partner—their wants, their needs, their expectations. Everything is about them and making sure that they are happy. It's incredibly disempowering and your whole sense of self and self-worth are shaken. So, as you navigate life post abuse and continue your healing journey, I invite you to be selfish and to make this process all about *you*. Give yourself permission to make *you* your number one priority. While this might initially feel uncomfortable or unnatural, I promise, it will get easier over time. You'll soon come to realize that investing in yourself isn't *selfish* but a means of self-preservation and self-empowerment.

In this chapter, I will support you in this self-empowerment process. You will have the opportunity to explore and reconnect with your core values and learn ways you can build yourself up. You will become familiar with your relationship rights and learn how to become more protective of yourself. And, finally, you will develop a greater understanding of what it means to be in a relationship that is balanced and supportive of your autonomy.

Finding Your Way Back to You

• Jasmine's Story

Jasmine had been out of her long-term, emotionally abusive relationship for almost a year. For, the most part, she was doing well. *Her mental health had significantly improved since being out of the relationship—she had more energy and felt less anxious. She had moved into a new apartment that she loved and was able to get back on track with her career goals. Things were on the up and up and she was feeling more hopeful about her future. Yet, despite these positive changes, Jasmine noticed that she still didn't feel like her old self.*

Before her relationship, Jasmine's life had been full. She was active and spent most weekends hiking. She was extremely social and liked meeting new people and making new friends. She was artistic and spent a lot of her free time making art and attending local art shows. However, when she met and became involved with her ex, her life drastically changed. Jasmine had become so consumed and emotionally drained by her relationship that she had little energy left for anything else. As a result, she became more withdrawn and stopped engaging in her hobbies. Jasmine missed this life that she had created for herself and realized she had lost herself to her relationship.

It's normal to feel lost and disconnected from the person you were before the abusive relationship. The good news is you can always find your way back to this person. You can start this process by reconnecting to your core values.

Reconnecting to Your Values

Your core values are the things you care strongly about and principles you stand by. These are the things that give your life meaning and purpose and shape your identity. Your values are also sources of motivation and inform your behavior. When you are living life in alignment with your core values or actively incorporating these values in your day-to-day life, you feel more confident and secure in who you are. This leads to feelings of self-assurance in the decisions you make, the goals you set, and the relationships you are in. Below are some examples of core values:

Family • Connection • Career success • Financial stability • Spirituality • Social justice • Independence • Autonomy • Physical health • Healthy lifestyle • Education • Altruism • Kindness • Achievement • Spontaneity • Structure • Integrity • Honesty • Adaptability • Creativity • Learning • Compassion • Empathy • Faith • Leadership • Sustainable living • Music • Mental health • Strength • Individuality • Trust • Respect • Consistency • Diversity • Passion • Community • Beauty • Rest • Balance • Nature • Athleticism • Romance • Routine • Humor • Open-mindedness • Cultural identity • Personal growth

If you were asked, right now, "What are your core values?" how might you respond? Would this be an easy question or a more challenging one? If you find this question difficult or intimidating, you are not alone. When you've been in an abusive dynamic and have had to contort and change various aspects of yourself to appease your partner and avoid conflict, it's common to take on and adopt the values of your partner and neglect or lose sight of your own. Therefore, if you feel unsure or disconnected from your values, that's okay. Now is the time to reacquaintance yourself with these values.

Exercise: Clarifying and Recommitting to Your Core Values

1. Set aside some time to think about and explore your core values—the things that matter most to *you*. You can use the following questions to help you gain some clarity:

    - "What's important to me?"

    - "What makes me feel fulfilled or gives my life meaning?"

    - "What did I care about or value before my relationship?"

- "What are some of my core values that I may have neglected or abandoned while I was in my relationship?"

    Write these values down in a journal or on a piece of paper. If you are still feeling stuck, use the list above as a reference.

2. For each value you have identified, write down *why* it's important to you.

    Example: *I value kindness because it helps me feel connected to others and I enjoy making other people feel good.*

    Example: *I value learning because I like to challenge myself and gain knowledge.*

3. Next, identify two to three values that you would like to prioritize and incorporate in your day-to-day life. Make a plan and identify what you will do to make this happen.

    Example: *Kindness—I will commit to doing one act of kindness every day (i.e., complimenting another person, holding the door open for someone).*

    Example: *Learning—I will sign up for a weekly Spanish class at the local community college.*

4. Maintain a daily or weekly log to hold yourself accountable and track your progress. Every time you engage in an activity that reinforces a core value, log it and note how you feel.

    Example: *Monday: I offered to help my older neighbor with her groceries. It felt good and I could tell that she appreciated the help.*

    Example: *Wednesday: I took my first Spanish class. At first, I was nervous, but I left the class feeling excited and am glad I signed up.*

If this exercise proves to be challenging or you are experiencing feelings of indecision, give yourself some time and space—it doesn't have to be completed in a single sitting. While this exercise is intended to help you clarify and recommit to your core values, remember, this is a process. Also, keep in mind that your values can shift and change. As you evolve and have more life experiences, your values are likely to reflect this evolution.

Building Yourself Up

In addition to reconnecting with your values, it's also important that you take the time to build yourself back up and reinforce your self-worth. When you can get to a place where you truly believe that your worth is inherent—not conditional or tied to your relationship status—you'll notice that you naturally become your own cheerleader and protector. You will be more kind and encouraging toward yourself and stand up for and assert yourself in situations that may have been difficult for you in the past. So, how do you build yourself up? Here's a good place to start:

1. **Surround yourself with people who build you up.** These are the people who accept you, respect you, celebrate you, and appreciate you. By being more mindful of who you choose to spend your time with and making a conscious effort to invest in healthy and meaningful relationships, you will start to feel more comfortable in your own skin and accepting of yourself.

    Examples: *Close friends, safe and loving family members, a supportive group or community*

2. **Engage in regular self-care.** Self-care can be considered as any activity that is restorative and nurturing of your mental health. When you consistently engage in activities that make you feel good, you are subconsciously reinforcing the belief "I am worthy."

    Examples: *An evening skin care routine, spending time outside and in nature, being around your pet, going to therapy, taking yourself on a dinner date*

3. **Continue to practice self-compassion.** Treat yourself with kindness and understanding. Hold space for and validate your feelings and offer yourself loving words when you are struggling.

   Examples: *Telling yourself, "It's okay, you're human" if you spill something, allowing yourself to have a good cry when you are struggling*

4. **Compliment and affirm yourself.** Do this by engaging in more positive self-talk and reminding yourself of how great you are and all the positive qualities you have. If this feels difficult, try thinking about some of the compliments your friends or loved ones have given you, or ask yourself, "What are the things my friends and loved ones like or appreciate about me?"

   Examples: *Recite daily affirmations, compliment yourself in front of the mirror each morning as you get ready for the day*

In this next exercise, using the methods above, you will have an opportunity to create an action plan that will help you build yourself back up.

Exercise: Making an Action Plan

When you were in the abusive relationship, your values and beliefs didn't change overnight—they changed gradually. Pivoting back to who you once were requires dedicated practice. Make an action plan to help you reengage with your values and create a life that is meaningful to *you*.

1. **Reconnect with or rebuild your support system.** Identify who is in your support system and two things you will do to nurture these relationships and connections in the next week.

   Example: *Support system: my sister and best friend. Plan: I will start calling my sister on my drive home from work and my best friend to schedule monthly dinner dates.*

2. **Create a self-care routine.** Come up with at least two self-care activities you can engage in on a daily basis. Come up with a specific plan that will facilitate this daily practice.

   Example: *Self-care activities: walks around my neighborhood, lighting a scented candle. Plan: I will start going on morning walks before work. I will set a reminder on my phone to light my candle in the evening.*

3. **Practice self-compassion regularly.** Come up with a self-compassion statement or affirmation you can use when you are struggling, feeling insecure, or down on yourself. Identify the steps you will take to ensure that you are using this self-compassion statement on a regular basis.

   Example: *Self-compassion statement: "It's okay to feel how you are feeling. You've been through a lot and it's going to take time to heal and feel like yourself again." Plan: I will put this statement on a notecard and hang it up on my bathroom mirror as a reminder.*

4. **Give yourself daily pep talks.** Identify an insecurity or something that you internally struggle with. Write yourself a pep talk (a short and encouraging speech) that you can read daily to affirm yourself and hype yourself up. Identify the steps you will take to integrate this pep talk into your daily routine.

   Example: *Insecurity: That I will never be in a healthy relationship. Pep talk: You were in a bad relationship, but your past does not have to dictate your future! You are an amazing person. You have so many wonderful qualities. You are smart, kind, and funny. And now you know what type of relationship you want and deserve and will never settle for anything less than that. Plan: I will keep this pep talk in the back of my journal and read it every night before I go to bed.*

Consistency and self-accountability are crucial to your healing. Use this action plan to help you stay on track and do the things you need to do to build yourself back up. You've got this!

Becoming Your Own Protector

While emotionally abusive relationships are devastating, you can use the experience to inform you of what you want and don't want in a future relationship. Now you know what an abusive relationship looks like and the red flags that indicate problematic or abusive behaviors. Now you know what your limits are and what you are not willing to tolerate or put up with. And now you know that just because you are in a relationship it doesn't mean you have to automatically relinquish your rights—the rights that you, like everyone else, are entitled to in every single one of your relationships. Below are your relationship rights that you *will* protect and honor moving forward:

Your Relationship Rights

1. **The right to feel safe—physically, emotionally, and mentally:** You have the right to feel comfortable and at ease. This also means that you have the right to end a relationship or leave a situation at any time and at any stage of the relationship if you feel unsafe.

2. **The right to change your mind:** You have the right to make a decision or have an opinion and then change your mind. You have the right to have new thoughts and new limits.

3. **The right to communicate your needs:** You have the right to express your needs without fear of judgment and consequence. Your needs are just as important as your partner, friend, and family member's needs.

4. **The right to personal time and space:** You have the right to take time for yourself and have a life outside of your

relationship. You have the right to take time for rest, to take care of your personal needs, and to do things that bring you joy and give your life meaning. You have the right to a balanced life.

5. **The right to your own identity and autonomy:** You have the right to an identity and life outside of your relationships. You have the right to determine your own identity based on what feels authentic to you. You have the right to your own values, beliefs, and lifestyle.

6. **The right to your own feelings:** You have the right to have your own feelings and to have your feelings respected. Your feelings are yours and reflect your inner experience. You do not have to justify or minimize your feelings for the sake of others.

When you have a strong understanding of your rights, you become a lot more inclined to protect your rights and feel more confident in your ability to assert these rights with others. In this next exercise, you are going to write a "Vows to Self" letter—a letter that reinforces your commitment to *you* and protecting yourself in future relationships.

Exercise: Vows to Self

Write a letter that states your commitment to yourself. Write this letter with the intention of instilling confidence in yourself and your ability to protect yourself and your relationship rights in the future. First, describe what you want in your next relationship and how you want to feel. Then, describe the actions you will take to protect yourself from future harm or abuse. Like the Loving Letter Exercise, if you are finding this exercise challenging, use the template below as a guide, which can be found at http://www.newharbinger.com/55480.

Vows to Self Template

Dear (your name here),

I am so proud of you. You put yourself first and have decided that you are going to do things differently moving forward. Now, you will only accept healthy love and relationships that are respectful and safe. Your next relationship will be (list qualities you desire in your future relationship, such as "supportive," "equitable," etc.) and you will feel (list desired feelings here, such as "safe," "comfortable," etc.).

You will be loyal to yourself and more protective of yourself. You will not tolerate any unkind or abusive behaviors from anyone. If a prospective partner (or anyone else in your life) does something hurtful or tries to harm you in any way, you will do one of the following things:

- Example: *Set firm boundaries immediately.*
- Example: *End the relationship.*

Remember, just like everyone else, you deserve a healthy relationship—a relationship that makes you feel safe, secure, and accepted.

Love,

(your name here)

Once you have written your letter, make sure that you have easy access to it. Go back to this letter and read it regularly as a reminder of your commitment to yourself, your safety, and your well-being.

Finding Balance and Doing You

Now that you have recommitted to yourself, it's time to plan for success! After being in a relationship that is codependent and all-consuming, now, more than ever, you desire a more balanced and harmonious relationship. And this is all very possible and within reach!

Shifting from Codependent to Interdependent

In emotionally abusive relationships, there is a culture of codependency. In this codependent dynamic, you become obsessive about your partner and engage in compulsive helping and caretaking (Beattie 2022). Your whole life and sense of self is caught up in this other person, and your well-being is dependent on theirs—which of course, as you now know, is not a sustainable way to exist. Therefore, to fulfill this desire for a balanced and harmonious relationship, you have to shift from a codependent mindset to an *interdependent* mindset.

In an interdependent relationship, you and your partner are equals and mutually invested in one another and the relationship. There is a shared understanding that both individuals will respond to the needs of the other only at "appropriate times and in the proper circumstances" (Mellody 2003). This means that having an interdependent mindset involves recognizing that your well-being is just as important as your partner's and not falling into the pattern of sacrificing your own needs to appease the other person or keep them happy.

To facilitate this shift, you need to actively practice communicating and asserting your needs and boundaries. If this concept feels foreign or even thinking about it makes you feel uncomfortable, lean into that. Be curious. Ask yourself, "Why does speaking my truth bring up anxiety?" Maybe it's fear of rejection and being disliked. Maybe you don't think your voice matters. Or maybe you are worried about letting someone else down. Whatever the reason, I hope you find the courage to speak up and stand up for yourself. There could be (and probably will be) some pushback from others who aren't used to you setting limits or being vocal. There is the possibility of fallout. But over time, you will feel more self-empowered and at peace for standing your ground and honoring yourself.

Here are some small but meaningful ways you can start practicing assertiveness and speaking your truth:

1. When someone gets your coffee order wrong, ask for the correct drink.
2. Set a small boundary at work. For example, if a coworker asks for a favor but your plate is full, politely inform them, "I'm sorry, now is not a good time for me."
3. Express an opposing or unpopular opinion to a friend. This could be an opinion about the ending of a television series or a dislike of a specific food.
4. Ask to reschedule plans if you aren't feeling well.

By starting small, with these "low stakes" situations, asserting yourself will feel a little bit more manageable. The reaction will typically be very benign—if any. You might get an eye roll or a huff—but you will survive, I promise. Keep going. Changing our behavior takes time and repetition, especially when we are doing something that we have little experience doing. But, the more you practice, the less painful it will feel. This next exercise will help you develop this skill.

Exercise: Everyday Assertiveness

Being assertive can be difficult, especially if it's a skill you were never taught. Below is a list of scenarios that can occur in your everyday life. As you read through the scenarios, consider how you would assert yourself and either express a need or set a boundary. If you would like, you can write these assertive statements or phrases on a piece of paper or in your journal for future reference and use.

- Your friend asks you to dinner, but you have had a long day at work and would like to go home and rest.

    Example of an assertive statement for this scenario: *"I'm sorry, it's been a long day, and I am going to need a raincheck."*

- You dread visiting your parents for the holidays because they always insist on talking about politics, which always escalates and results in an argument.

    Example of an assertive statement: *"I am going to ask that we not talk about politics over the weekend. If it does get brought up, I am going to have to take some space and go into another room until the conversation is over."*

- You are given the wrong food or drink order.

    Example of an assertive statement: *"Excuse me, I ordered X, but this is Y. May I please have X?"*

- You disagree with the perspective or sentiment of a close friend on a specific topic.

    Example of an assertive statement: *"I actually don't feel the same way and have a different opinion. I think _____."*

- You are uncomfortable with your coworkers gossiping about another coworker at lunch.

    Example of an assertive statement: *"I don't feel comfortable talking about this other person when they are not here, so I'm going to remove myself from this conversation."*

When you start asserting yourself in low-stake situations, you'll find that it becomes easier and more natural over time. You'll soon realize, despite the brief discomfort, that speaking up for yourself or setting limits is quite empowering.

Creating a Balanced Life

As you have learned, relationships do not have to be all-consuming. In fact, relationships thrive when both partners have their own identities, lives, and interests independent of the relationship and partner. Therefore, creating a balanced life is crucial for your own mental health and well-being and the well-being of your future relationship. So, how do you achieve this balance? Here are some tips to help you create a balanced life moving forward:

- **Maintain your personal commitments:** Try to avoid changing your plans or preexisting commitments for the sake of a partner or relationship. Communicate the importance of these commitments to your partner or prospective partner.

- **Nurture your personal relationships:** Continue to invest in your friendships and the other important relationships in your life. Communicate the importance of these relationships to your partner or prospective partner.

- **Commit to your hobbies and passions:** Continue to engage in the things that bring you joy and give your life meaning and purpose outside of your relationship. Communicate the importance of having a life and identity outside of your relationship with your partner or prospective partner.

- **Show up authentically:** Embrace every part of you—your strengths, your quirks, your flaws, your beliefs, and your values—and only seek out relationships that are accepting of this authentic version of you.

Let's Recap

Losing yourself in an emotionally abusive relationship is common. When you are in an abusive dynamic, your needs and well-being become second to the abuser's needs and well-being. However, by reconnecting to and honoring your core values, learning how to become more protective of yourself, shifting to an interdependent mindset, and creating a life that is balanced and a reflection of who you are and what you want, you can take your power back and return to yourself.

Conclusion: Moving Forward with Intention

Emotionally abusive relationships are so many things. They are perplexing, exhausting, devastating, and all-consuming. They make you question yourself—your worth, your judgment, your values—and take a huge toll on your mental health and well-being. However, you picked up this book and started your healing journey because something deep inside you *knew* that this was not the relationship you wanted or deserved. And now, you have the tools to break free.

You learned what makes a relationship healthy and what makes a relationship abusive. You learned about the emotionally abusive partner—their personality, their patterns of behaviors, and why it is highly unlikely that they will ever change. You learned how the emotionally abusive relationship can affect you and compromise other areas of your life and functioning, and why you might be avoiding confronting the reality of the abusive dynamic. You learned about the effort that is required of you to end a relationship with an emotionally abusive partner and the importance of asserting yourself and maintaining firm boundaries. And you learned about the role of trauma and grief post abuse, the steps you can take to heal from this traumatic experience, and how you can take your power back and live a life that is authentic and meaningful to you.

While this might be the end of the book, it might not necessarily be the end of your healing journey. Recovering from abuse and breaking old habits often takes time—and that's okay! Even if you are not ready to take the leap and leave your relationship, know that this is *your* process: you have to do it on *your* terms. You can always come back to this book for guidance and support. Most importantly, as you continue to move through your healing, try to be patient with yourself and continue to practice self-compassion. You are doing the very best you can and are going to come out the other side—as I and so many others have.

You can and will get through this.

Acknowledgments

I would like to take a moment to thank those individuals who have been instrumental and impactful in the process of creating this book.

To New Harbinger Publications, thank you for taking on this project and believing in the mission of this book—to guide and empower individuals to break free and heal from emotionally abusive relationships. Thank you to my editors, Georgia Kolias and Beth Bolton, for your enthusiasm, investment, and hard work.

To my clients, past and present, thank you for sharing your experiences with me. It has been an honor to work with you. I admire your resilience and commitment to healing.

To my friends, family, and life partner who have supported and encouraged me throughout this entire endeavor, thank you.

To my writing coach, Marni Freedman, thank you for all of your guidance and for empowering me to find my voice.

To my clinical supervisors and peers throughout the years, thank you for providing a positive and collaborative working environment. I am forever grateful for our consultations.

To the people who have been so generous with their time to read and review this book, thank you. I know your time is valuable and am grateful for your support.

References

Beattie, M. 2022. *Codependent No More: How to Stop Controlling Others and Start Caring for Yourself*. New York: Spiegel & Grau.

Bernheim, D., A. Buchheim, M. Domin, R. Mentel, and M. Lotze. 2022. "Neural Correlates of Attachment Representation in Patients with Borderline Personality Disorder Using a Personalized Functional Magnetic Resonance Imaging Task," *Frontiers in Human Neuroscience* 16: 810417, https://doi.org/10.3389/fnhum.2022.810417.

Cozolino, L. J. 2014. *The Neuroscience of Human Relationships: Attachment and the Developing Social Brain*. New York: W. W. Norton & Company.

Dichter, M. E., K. A. Thomas, P. Crits-Christoph, S. N. Ogden, and K. V. Rhodes. 2018. "Coercive Control in Intimate Partner Violence: Relationship with Women's Experience of Violence, Use of Violence, and Danger," *Psychology of Violence* 8: 596–604, https://doi.org/10.1037/vio0000158.

Domestic Abuse Intervention Programs. n.d. "Equality Wheel," https://www.theduluthmodel.org/wp-content/uploads/2017/03/Equality.pdf.

Gibson, L. C. 2015. *Adult Children of Emotionally Immature Parents: How to Heal from Distant, Rejecting, or Self-Involved Parents*. Oakland, CA: New Harbinger Publications.

Harris, R. 2008. *The Happiness Trap*. London: Robinson Publishing.

Levine, A., and R. Heller. 2011. *Attached: The New Science of Adult Attachment and How It Can Help You Find—and Keep—Love*. New York: Jeremy P. Tarcher.

Mellody, P. 2003. *Facing Codependence: What It Is, Where It Comes From, How It Sabotages Our Lives*. New York: HarperCollins.

Morris, L. S., M. M. Grehl, S. B. Rutter, M. Mehta, and M. L. Westwater. 2022. "What Motivates Us: A Detailed Review of Intrinsic v. Extrinsic Motivation," *Psychological Medicine* 52: 1801–1816, https://doi.org/10.1017/S0033291722001611.

National Academies of Sciences, Engineering, and Medicine. 2018. *Addressing the Social and Cultural Norms That Underlie the Acceptance of Violence: Proceedings of a Workshop—in Brief.* Washington, DC: National Academies Press, https://doi.org/10.17226/2507.

Paetzold, R. L., W. S. Rholes, and J. L. Kohn. 2015. "Disorganized Attachment in Adulthood: Theory, Measurement, and Implications for Romantic Relationships," *Review of General Psychology* 19: 146–156, http://doi.org/10.137/gpr0000042.

Parnell, L. 2008. *Tapping In: A Step-by-Step Guide to Activating Your Healing Resources Through Bilateral Stimulation.* Boulder, CO: Sounds True.

Shapiro, F. 2012. *Getting Past Your Past: Take Control of Your Life with Self-Help Techniques from EMDR Therapy.* New York: Rodale.

Shapiro, F. 2018. *Eye Movement Desensitization and Reprocessing (EMDR) Therapy, Third Edition: Basic Principles, Protocols, and Procedures.* New York: Guilford.

Sharpley, C. F. 2009. "Neurobiological Pathways Between Chronic Stress and Depression: Dysregulated Adaptive Mechanisms?" *Clinical Medicine Insights: Psychiatry* 2. doi:10.4137/CMPsy.S3658.

Sprecher, S., and D. Felmlee. 2021. "Social Network Pressure on Women and Men to Enter a Romantic Relationship and Fear of Being Single," *Interpersona: An International Journal on Personal Relationships* 15: 246–261, https://doi.org/10.5964/ijpr.6139.

Stewart, R., B. Wright, L. Smith, S. Roberts, and N. Russell. 2021. "Gendered Stereotypes and Norms: A Systematic Review of Interventions Designed to Shift Attitudes and Behaviour," *Heliyon* 7: e06660, https://doi.org/10.1016/j.heliyon.2021.e06660.

van der Kolk, B. 2014. *The Body Keeps the Score: Brain, Mind, and Body in the Healing of Trauma.* New York: Penguin.

van Nieuwenhove, K., and R. Meganck. 2017. "Interpersonal Features in Complex Trauma Etiology, Consequences, and Treatment: A Literature Review," *Journal of Aggression, Maltreatment & Trauma* 28: 903–928, https://doi.org/10.1080/10926771.2017.1405316.

Leah Aguirre, LCSW, is a licensed clinical social worker practicing in San Diego, CA. She works primarily with individuals who have experienced complex trauma, including childhood abuse, domestic violence, and dating violence; and provides trauma-based treatment, including eye movement desensitization and reprocessing (EMDR). Aguirre contributes to *Psychology Today*, and has been featured in major media such as *Bumble*, *GQ*, *Reader's Digest*, and *Hello Giggles*.

Foreword writer **Avery Neal, PhD, LPC**, is a practicing psychotherapist, international author and speaker, and founder of the Women's Therapy Clinic in Houston, TX, which offers psychiatric and counseling support to women. She is author of *If He's So Great, Why Do I Feel So Bad?*.

Real change *is* possible

For more than fifty years, New Harbinger has published proven-effective self-help books and pioneering workbooks to help readers of all ages and backgrounds improve mental health and well-being, and achieve lasting personal growth. In addition, our spirituality books offer profound guidance for deepening awareness and cultivating healing, self-discovery, and fulfillment.

Founded by psychologist Matthew McKay and Patrick Fanning, New Harbinger is proud to be an independent, employee-owned company. Our books reflect our core values of integrity, innovation, commitment, sustainability, compassion, and trust. Written by leaders in the field and recommended by therapists worldwide, New Harbinger books are practical, accessible, and provide real tools for real change.

MORE BOOKS from NEW HARBINGER PUBLICATIONS

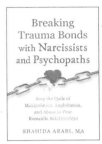

BREAKING TRAUMA BONDS WITH NARCISSISTS AND PSYCHOPATHS

Stop the Cycle of Manipulation, Exploitation, and Abuse in Your Romantic Relationships

978-1648483561 / US $19.95

STOP WALKING ON EGGSHELLS FOR PARTNERS

What to Do When Your Partner Has Borderline or Narcissistic Personality Disorder

978-1608824878 / US $19.95

THE DBT WORKBOOK FOR NARCISSISTIC ABUSE AND GASLIGHTING

Dialectical Behavior Therapy Skills to Stay Emotionally Centered, Overcome Self-Doubt, and Reclaim Your Self-Worth

978-1648482892 / US $25.95

ADULT CHILDREN OF EMOTIONALLY IMMATURE PARENTS

How to Heal from Distant, Rejecting, or Self-Involved Parents

978-1626251700 / US $18.95

LETTING GO OF YOUR EX

CBT Skills to Heal the Pain of a Breakup and Overcome Love Addiction

978-1648480379 / US $20.95

THE BETTER BOUNDARIES GUIDED JOURNAL

A Safe Space to Reflect on Your Needs and Work Toward Healthy, Respectful Relationships

978-1648482755 / US $19.95

newharbingerpublications
1-800-748-6273 / newharbinger.com

(VISA, MC, AMEX / prices subject to change without notice)

Follow Us 🔘 🅕 𝕏 ▶ ⓟ 𝗂𝗇 ♪ ⓖ

Don't miss out on new books from New Harbinger.
Subscribe to our email list at **newharbinger.com/subscribe**

Did you know there are **free tools** you can download for this book?

Free tools are things like **worksheets, guided meditation exercises**, and **more** that will help you get the most out of your book.

You can download free tools for this book—whether you bought or borrowed it, in any format, from any source—from the New Harbinger website. All you need is a NewHarbinger.com account. Just use the URL provided in this book to view the free tools that are available for it. Then, click on the "download" button for the free tool you want, and follow the prompts that appear to log in to your NewHarbinger.com account and download the material.

You can also save the free tools for this book to your **Free Tools Library** so you can access them again anytime, just by logging in to your account! Just look for this button on the book's free tools page.

+ Save this to my free tools library

If you need help accessing or downloading free tools, visit **newharbinger.com/faq** or contact us at **customerservice@newharbinger.com**.